YOU ARE HEALED OF THE LORD

Copyright © 2021 by
Rogina Gale
LCCN: 2021921069

All rights reserved.
This book, or parts thereof, may not be
reproduced in any form without permission.

Paperback ISBN: 978-1-63337-563-5
E-Book ISBN: 978-1-63337-564-2

Printed in the United States of America
1 3 5 7 9 10 8 6 4 2

YOU ARE HEALED OF THE LORD

ROGINA GALE

I dedicate this book to my family; Zacchari, Andrew, Pamela, and Naomi. May you continue to seek the wisdom of the Lord and always know and feel your Heavenly Father's overwhelming love for you.

ACKNOWLEDGEMENTS

I would like to first thank my Heavenly Father for His overwhelming love, care, and continual faithfulness to share His love and wisdom. I would also like to thank my mom, Pamela King aka Nanna, for the hours of editing. And my sons, Zacchari and Andrew and daughter-in-love, Naomi, for your constant love, encouragement, and input. I am so blessed to have such a wonderful family. To my publisher, for your patience through this writing process.

TABLE OF CONTENTS

Chapter 1 – Healing is a Process – Follow the Leading of the Lord 1

Chapter 2 – Guard Your Heart and Mind 17

Chapter 3 – The Seed of His Word 27

Chapter 4 – Your Rights & Privileges as a Child of God 39

Chapter 5 – Some Reasons People May Not Be Receiving Healing 49

Chapter 6 – The Power of Fasting 79

Chapter 7 – Scriptures to Stand on for Any Healing Need 85

Chapter 8 – Scriptures to Stand on for Specific Areas of Healing of Your Physical Body 91

Chapter 9 – Scriptures to Stand on for Specific Areas of Healing for Your Mind, Will, And Emotions. 105

Chapter 10 – Scripture Lists Referred to Throughout the Book 119

INTRODUCTION

HAVE YOU EVER NEEDED or known someone who needed healing in some area of their life? We all have. Healing can be needed in our physical bodies, minds (thoughts and ways of thinking), will, emotions, relationship with God, relationships with others, habits, lifestyles, behaviors, or finances, to name a few. There is always something in ours or other's lives that needs the Lord's touch.

Every answer we need has been written down for us by the Lord in His Holy Word, the Bible. These are His promises to us. No matter the need or situation we face, God is right there waiting for us to run to His open arms. He wants to wrap His loving arms around us so we can feel His love, hope, and encouragement. The Lord wants to give us wisdom, guidance, and direction. He has the answer to *everything* we need.

Some healings are true miracles, instantaneous. Yet, most healings are a process that takes place over time. These healings take standing in faith and some action on our part. Since we each have different healing needs, we each need to seek God for the process He wants us to follow toward that healing.

For every healing process, we must remember God loves us all unconditionally. He *wants* us to be healed and whole. The power of God's Word *will* work in our lives as we place our faith in it. We are to keep seeking Him, listening to Him, spending time in His presence through prayer, reading of His Word, and worshiping Him, keeping our minds, hearts, homes, and surroundings filled with the things of God.

In this book, I will share what I have learned while seeking God for my own healing needs. I will concentrate on God's promises regarding healing of our physical bodies, minds, wills, and emotions.

This book is designed as a reference book. Chapters 1-6 cover the things the Lord has shown me as I was seeking Him for my healing. In Chapters 7-9, I have listed scriptures for you to stand on as you trust God to bring to pass your healing. The scriptures are categorized alphabetically according to the area of need.

Even though I have spent many years accumulating the scripture references, I know there are many more to be found. That is why it is important for each of us to study the Word. You may find that one specific scripture that will change your heart and life forever.

INTRODUCTION

As you read these pages, I pray you will be encouraged, strengthened in your faith, filled with hope, be at peace, and that there will be no fear. I also pray that as your faith increases, every need in your life will be met. I challenge you to stand strong in the Lord and in the power of His might. Seek Him, trust Him, love Him, and let Him love you in return.

Look up the scriptures in your Bible, and mark them. The Word of God is so vast with many treasures. You could study it your whole life, learn something new every day, and still not reach the end of all that it contains.

SEARCH, SEEK, STUDY, DIG, and
FIND HIS TREASURES!

CHAPTER 1
HEALING IS A PROCESS – FOLLOW THE LEADING OF THE LORD

BEFORE WE BEGIN, I would like to pray.

"Dear precious, Heavenly Father, we love You. We thank You for Your overwhelming love, mercy, and grace toward us. We come to You in the mighty name of Jesus. We thank You that Your power and anointing are upon Your Word, and our hearts are open to receive what You have for us. I thank you, Father, that everyone who reads these pages will be encouraged, filled with hope, and be strengthened by You to stand strong in their faith until they see Your Word fulfilled in their lives. We believe that as we pray, Your Word does not go up unto You void as it says in Isaiah 55:11. Your Word will be accomplished. We confess we will not look to the left or the right but will keep our eyes fixed on You, the Author and Finisher of our faith. Thank You for Your strength to do so. You are so faithful. We love and adore You. In the precious name of Jesus, we pray. Amen."

YOU ARE HEALED OF THE LORD

As we go through life, we have all experienced times when we needed healing or the Lord's touch in some area or have known someone in need. There are many areas of our lives that can need healing, not just in our physical bodies, but our minds (thoughts and ways of thinking), will, emotions, relationship with God, relationships with others, habits, lifestyles, behaviors, or finances. The list can go on and on.

As you read the Bible, you will find that the Lord has written the answers down for us in His Holy Word. It holds His promises to us. God's promises are a contract He offers us - a Holy covenant. This contract was signed and sealed with the blood and death of His dear, precious Son, Jesus Christ. His promises are for every one of His children. We have to choose to trust Him to fulfill them in our lives. No matter the problem or concern, big or small, God's Word will never fail. It may not be instantaneous, but it will not fail. God is always true to His Word. God sees no impossibilities. *With Him, ALL things are possible* (Matthew 19:26).

Some healings are true miracles - instantaneous. These healings stir peoples' faith. We praise and thank the Lord for those. But most healings are a process that we walk through. The process of healing that God has for one person may not be exactly the same process He has for another. We each need to seek God to reveal our own

CHAPTER 1: HEALING IS A PROCESS

individual process for our healing. There are some aspect of the healing process that are the same for everyone such as:

1. God loves us all very much. He *wants* us to be healed and whole in every area of our lives.

2. The power of the Word *does* work.

3. We are to continue seeking Him, listening to Him, spending time in His presence through prayer, the reading of His Word, and worshipping Him.

4. We must confess His promises (speaking His Word) about our situation.

5. We are to trust Him to fulfill His Word.

6. We must do what we can do to keep our minds, hearts, homes, and surroundings filled with what is of the Lord.

You may say, "*My need is so big. I don't see how it can get better.*" God is able to take care of any size need. If He *created the world and all that is in it* (Genesis 1:1, Psalms 33:6, 9), is anything too big for Him? Psalms 46:6 says, "*He uttered His voice, the earth melted.*" If He can melt the earth with His voice, is helping you too hard for Him? If

YOU ARE HEALED OF THE LORD

He created the world and all that is in it just by speaking, is helping you too much for Him? Is anything too hard for your God? No! It is nothing for Him. Besides, He WANTS to help you. He LOVES to help you. You are His child.

You may also say, "*My need is small and insignificant. God's not concerned with my need.*" If God cares to know how many hairs are on your head (Matthew 10:30), He cares about the smallest problem or concern. It is His desire and pleasure to help us. He wants to be a part of every area of our lives. He wants to be our Abba Father (our Daddy), our best friend, our provider, and our healer - our everything.

You may say, "*I do not deserve the Lord's help.*" God loves you so much. God knows our struggles, including the negative thoughts and emotions with which we fight. Even while we were yet sinners, God sent His Only Son, Jesus Christ, to die for us (Romans 5:8). He knowingly allowed and put His Son through this for YOU. Jesus was stripped of all His glory, honor, position, home, family, and friends both in heaven and on earth. Every sickness, disease, and plague known and those that were not yet known, and every sin were placed upon Him in front of everyone. He was humiliated, spit on, beaten with a whip that was covered with sharp objects, beard ripped out, and nailed to a cross. He endured all this for you, so

CHAPTER 1: HEALING IS A PROCESS

that you could be free and have victory in every area of your life.

Isaiah 53:5 says, "*By the stripes of Jesus we are healed.*" Jesus received exactly 39 stripes on His back. Jewish law said that each person that was to receive stripes was to receive "*40 stripes save one*" (II Corinthians 11:24). I wondered why 39 stripes? What is the meaning? While studying the meaning of numbers, I learned that the number 39 is the number for disease. The number 30 is the number of consecration, the blood of Christ, and the perfection of divine order. The number 9 is the number of divine completeness from the Lord, the conclusion of a matter. So with 39 stripes, Jesus completely covered our sickness and disease with His blood and brought back perfection, completely, forever, concluding the matter. That is why it says, "*By His stripes we were healed*" (I Peter 2:24). It is already done. Hallelujah! "*It is finished!*" (John 19:30). He did that all for you and me. What overwhelming love!

Oh, how much God loves us, and desires us to be healed. Since the beginning, God has been moving on behalf of and touching the lives of His creation. He desires that none of us should be lost, sick, diseased, sad, or hurting. God is waiting with His arms wide open for us to run into them. He wants to wrap His loving arms around us so that we can feel His love, hope, be encouraged, and He can give us wisdom, guidance, and direction. He has the answer to *everything* we need.

With that in mind, we can seek our healing process with confidence. We seek God's healing process for our life by spending time in prayer, listening for His voice, and looking up and studying scriptures on wisdom and guidance. (See Chapter 10 for scriptures on "Wisdom and Guidance in your Healing Process.") Speak those scriptures as you pray. The Lord tells us to put Him in remembrance of His Word. It is not that He has forgotten it, but is for us to remind ourselves of His promises, to increase our faith, and to give the angels of heaven commands to act on (Psalms 103:20). The Word is alive, powerful, and a creative force (Hebrews 4:12).

When you are seeking the Lord for your healing, listen for what He desires for you personally to do in your healing process and follow His leading. Be careful to not rely on what others have done in their process of healing. If we are only following what others are telling us to do, we can miss hearing the Lord's leading. This does not mean that the Lord will not have you do what others have done. Someone may share with you what they did in receiving their healing, and you will sense the Lord quicken your spirit that you should do the same.

Once I was having an issue with my stomach. The Lord had me fast breakfast for 30 days and spend the time I would be eating breakfast studying His Word. During

CHAPTER 1: HEALING IS A PROCESS

my time of healing, He also had me help in the children's ministry of our church. When the Lord first asked me to help in the children's ministry, I thought, "*How can I do that? My stomach hurts worse when I am up and about.*" But the Lord said, "*Do this, and your healing will come.*" As I obeyed Him, my healing came.

If you feel you have not heard from the Lord with any specific instructions He wants you to do in your healing process, then just keep speaking and standing on His written Word. This may be all that He wants you to do! Speaking His Word is always part of every process. His Word never fails. Isaiah 55:11 says that *His Word does not go up to Him void.* If you study verses on the power and authority of God and His Word, you will see and know the power and authority of God and His Word. Then keep praying and seeking Him. *God is able and willing to help!* (See Chapter 10 for scriptures on "Power and Authority of God and His Word.")

"*Peace, be still*" (Mark 4:39). These are powerful words to stand on for *any* storm you are going through. Many times in my life, I have spoken that scripture over myself or situation, such as times when my mind was not being quiet, pain and cramping in my body, a stomachache, and many other situations where peace was needed. I have laid my hands on my children's stomach and my own and said, "*I command you, stomach, in the name of Jesus, to be at peace and be still.*" If your mind won't be quiet, tell it, "*Peace, be still in the name of Jesus.*" You can use this scripture for any storm in your life.

Now if you don't see immediate results don't say, "It did not help (or work)." Daniel prayed for 21 days before the answer came (Daniel 10:8-14). This does not mean it will take 21 days for your answer to come, but to show you not to give up until your answer comes. Keep speaking the Word and believing it. Speaking the Word also builds faith in your heart. "*Faith comes by hearing and hearing the Word of the Lord*" (Romans 10:17). Hold onto your faith like a bulldog! If you look at a bulldog, his nose is set back on his head. This is so that when it gets into fights, it can lock onto what it is fighting without its nose being covered so that it can still breathe. When a bulldog is in a fight, it does not let go until it wins. God gave us the Holy Spirit and His Word to have the strength to fight and to keep us in the fight so that we don't give up and can hold on until the victory comes.

Luke 11:5-8 Jesus gave us an example of not giving up until we get our answer. In this example, the man kept knocking on his neighbor's door late at night in need of bread for a guest. He knocked until he got what he needed. Jesus ended the story with,

> *"If a son shall ask bread of any of you that is a father, will he give him a stone? If ye then being evil know how to give good gifts unto your children, how*

CHAPTER 1: HEALING IS A PROCESS

much more shall your Heavenly Father give good gifts unto them that ask?" (Luke 11:11-13)

Genesis 32: 24-31 gives another example. Jacob held onto the messenger until he got the answer he wanted. God is good! He is not your enemy. As King David said in Psalms 27:13-14, "*I had fainted, unless I had believed to see the goodness of the Lord in the land of the living. Wait on the Lord: be of good courage, and He shall strengthen thine heart: wait, I say, on the Lord.*" Some of the wonderful benefits the goodness of God includes our healing, peace, mercy, grace, favor, and protection. (See Chapter 10 for scriptures on "Goodness of God.")

God is like a good shepherd. We are the sheep of His pasture (John 10:7-14). In nature, a lamb is not easily herded. If a sheep does not have a lot of handling by a human, they can scare very easily. They are much easier to care for if they can be led. They follow what they know and trust.

Just like a lamb needs to get to know its shepherd, we need to get to know our Good Shepherd and follow Him, not running around like scared sheep. Finding and reading scriptures on God being with us, answering prayers, and deliverance by God will encourage you in your desire to follow the Lord, our Good Shepherd. You will learn of the goodness of God, how He is with His children

YOU ARE HEALED OF THE LORD

(you), how He hears your prayers, and that He answers your prayers with deliverance and victory. (See Chapter 10 for scriptures on "Answering Prayers," "Deliverance by God," and "God Being with Us.")

We need to wake up every day expecting good things and to hear God's voice. If you are not in a habit of thinking and expecting good things or hearing God's voice, it can take effort and work. This is a daily walk and a choice. We grow in this expectation and ability by spending time with God in prayer and in the Word.

The Word says *that only blessings shall follow you all the days of your life and that of your children for a thousand generations* (Deuteronomy 7:9). *Old things are passed away, and behold all things are new* (II Corinthians 5:17). You are a new creature in Christ Jesus. Remind yourself continually. Say to yourself, "*I have a new Daddy. I am like my Father.* (Say what your Heavenly Father is like.) *I am redeemed. I am blessed. All the days of my life, I am blessed. The Lord goes before me and fights for me* (Deuteronomy 1:30). *He is a shield around about me* (Psalms 3:3). *Who can come against me? No weapon formed against me shall prosper* (Isaiah 54:17). *No evil shall befall me* (Psalms 91:10). *The Lord, my refuge, is my habitation. God's truth, His word, is my shield and my buckler* (Psalms 18:2)."

Receive the goodness of the Lord! How do you receive the goodness of God and your healing? You *decide*

CHAPTER 1: HEALING IS A PROCESS

to accept it is yours as a child of God. How do you accept and take it? First, you believe it is yours. If you have made Jesus Lord of your life, then you are a child of God. As His child, everything in the Word is for you. Having child like faith is simply to trust and believe what God said He will do, He will do. When you tell a child you will get them something, they believe you and hold you to your word. They don't think, "Yah, right? We will see." They believe you. Second, you say you believe it is yours. Think about a little child who sees a toy that is theirs or that they want. They will begin saying, "Mine, Mine!" They will fight for the toy. They just know that it is theirs. The Word says that we are to have childlike faith. We are to claim (say aloud), believe, and stand firm that healing is ours (Mine, mine!), and whatever else the Word says is ours. **Hallelujah! The Lord loves you and desires to do good things in your life!**

The process toward healing is too great for us to do it alone. We need the strength that only comes from Heavenly Father. We need His touch daily. Just as you need to feed your physical body every day or you lose your strength, you need to feed your spirit daily or it will lose its strength. If we don't spend time daily with our loving, Heavenly Father through praying, praising and worshiping Him, reading, studying, meditating (thinking) on His Word, and listening to what our Heavenly

YOU ARE HEALED OF THE LORD

Father would say to us, we become discouraged and frustrated as we are walking out our healing. Without constant encounters with the Living God, we can become consumed with our battles, and we are no longer thinking about the promises of our Heavenly Father. We are then trying to obtain our healing in our own strength. You need the strength of the Lord to stay strong in the battle. If we are constantly distracted from spending time alone with the Lord, we will be isolated from the power and help that comes from God to overcome our battles. We are strengthened, protected, and every need provided by abiding or living continually in the Lord. Psalms 91 shows us this.

> *"He that dwelleth in the secret place of the most High shall abide under the shadow of the Almighty. I will say of the Lord, He is my refuge and my fortress: my God; in Him will I trust. Surely He shall deliver thee from the snare of the fowler, and from the noisome pestilence. He shall cover thee with His feathers, and under His wings shalt thou trust: His truth shall be thy shield and buckler. Thou shalt not be afraid for the terror by night; nor for the arrow that flieth by day; Nor for the pestilence that walketh in darkness; nor for the destruction that wasteth at noonday. A thousand*

CHAPTER 1: HEALING IS A PROCESS

shall fall at thy side, and ten thousand at thy right hand; but it shall not come nigh thee. Only with thine eyes shalt thou behold and see the reward of the wicked. Because thou hast made the Lord, which is my refuge, even the Most High, thy habitation; There shall no evil befall thee; neither shall any plague come nigh thy dwelling. For He shall give His angels charge over thee, to keep thee in all thy way. They shall bear thee up in their hands, lest thou dash thy food against a stone. Thou shalt tread upon the lion and adder: The young lion and the dragon shalt thou trample under feet. Because he hath set his love upon Me, therefore will I deliver him; I will set him on high, because he hath known My name. He shall call upon Me, and I will answer him: I will be with him in trouble; I will deliver him, and honor him. With long life will I satisfy him, and show him My salvation."

You may say, "I am too busy to spend time daily praying or reading the Word." Prayer can happen anywhere you are. How about when you are getting ready for the day, while in the shower, while getting dressed, in the car, doing chores, exercising, whatever you may be doing? You can also listen to teaching while doing these same activities and as you are falling asleep at night. As we

YOU ARE HEALED OF THE LORD

devote time to Him, He will help us with what we have to do each day. You will be amazed at how quickly you get things done and how they'll happen much easier as you make time with the Lord an important part of every day. *"The Lord is a rewarder of them that diligently seek Him"* (Hebrews 11:6).

Maybe you really are too busy. You may need to drop some activities from your schedule. Ask the Lord for wisdom. You could be involved with a lot, but that doesn't mean the activities are God's will for your lives. Ask Him for His perfect will for your life, what you should be involved in, and for wisdom in making time to spend with Him.

We really need to have undivided quiet times with the Lord. There are times I stay up after everyone has gone to bed, or I get up early. At times, I tell my family I need to go pray, and they give me time with the Lord. Sometimes, the Lord has awakened me in the middle of the night to spend time with Him. On occasion, you will feel the need or urgency on the inside to pray. If you can, stop what you are doing and pray. If you can't stop, pray while doing whatever you have to do. Do not ignore these feelings. That is the Lord calling you. You may miss something great or special that the Lord has for you, or you are needed to intercede for someone else's need. Be obedient. You will never regret it.

CHAPTER 1: HEALING IS A PROCESS

Don't be mistaken. If we ignore the Spirit's voice too much, we become hard of hearing and hardhearted. It is also hard to listen if you are always talking to the Lord and never quiet long enough to hear Him. Keep your hearing sharp by spending time with the Lord, listening for Him, and obeying His voice.

As you walk through this phase of your healing, finding your healing process, remember your Heavenly Father loves you dearly and it is His desire, heart, and will that you are healed.

CHAPTER 2

GUARD YOUR HEART AND MIND

WHEN THE LORD FIRST started showing me about each of us finding our own process of healing, I was seeking Him for my son's healing (who was a baby at the time). He was very sick the first several months of his life with constant and severe cold-like symptoms. The doctors were doing all they knew to do. Nothing they recommended was working. Because my son was so congested, I would lie awake many nights listening to his breathing, concerned that he would not be able to breathe from the congestion.

I started really seeking God as to why my son was not being healed. I was doing all I knew to do to see him healed. I knew to pray and speak the Word regarding the situation. The Lord then spoke to me about a TV program that I was watching. It had a gentleman on it who the Lord said was living a very ungodly lifestyle. (The Lord did not tell me any specifics of the lifestyle.) The Lord showed me that as I watched the program, by choice, I allowed the spirit that was upon this man's life into my home. I could not tell there was a spiritual problem by appearances, for the show was very innocent to look at and no issue was obvious with the man. I thanked the Lord for showing me this, and I asked Him to forgive me for allowing that into my home. I never turned that show on again. I prayed over my home, anointed it with oil, and asked the Lord to cleanse it of everything that was not of Him that I had allowed in through the television and other means. My son began to instantly improve.

This is when the Lord started teaching me that allowing certain things into my home and life allows the spirit that goes with it to enter into my home and life as well. It was as if I had opened the door and said, "*Come on in.*" Some of the gentleman's very immoral behavior came out later in the news. Unlike this program, many shows and objects are very obvious if they are ungodly. There is no doubt that witches, evil-looking creatures, magic, sorcery, ghosts, statues used to symbolize gods, demonic and cultic symbols, sexual immorality, other immoral acts, using the Lord's name in vain, etc., are ungodly. There are many scriptures that say what is "an abomination to the Lord" (Leviticus 20:13, Proverbs 6:16-19, Proverbs 17:15, Galatians 5:19-21, I Corinthians 6:9-11). Yet, like the program I was watching, there may be items and activities that you cannot see or are not easily seen like actors'/actress' lifestyles, demonic and cultic symbols that are on items, pictures, and statues in the background, or

CHAPTER 2: GUARD YOUR HEART AND MIND

whatever else the enemy tries to use. This is why we must listen to the Holy Spirit speaking to us.

At times, things can find their way into our home and life without us realizing it. They can come through innocent gifts, movies, TV, etc. This is why a house and life cleansing from time to time is needed. Regularly, ask the Lord to show you if there is anything in your home or life that needs to be removed.

When my children were young, there are times the Lord had me go through their rooms. He helped me find what was brought into our home through their innocence, and at times, their rebellion. The world will say that you are invading your children's privacy. This is a lie of the enemy. This is how Satan and the world can overtake our children. We must be watchful. It is our responsibility as parents to protect God's gifts, our children, as well as the atmosphere of our homes. I am not talking about being mean, nasty, and overbearing with them. In love, we are to set a standard in our home, stand firm, and raise them up in the nurture and admonition of the Lord - teaching them what is right and wrong. Spend time talking to your children, teaching them why you believe what you do, such as not allowing certain things into your home or life. You need to help them understand the importance of guarding our hearts and minds. They need to know why, so they can have the wisdom to make good choices themselves. Just saying, "*Because I said so,*" doesn't teach them but can make them feel disregarded, unloved, and uncared for and can breed rebellion.

Know that you are not alone in this process. Praise God, the Lord has given us a helper, an alarm system, the Holy Spirit. Jesus said in John 16:13, "*Howbeit when he, the Spirit of truth, is come, he will guide you into all truth: for he shall not speak of himself; but whatsoever he shall hear, that shall he speak: and he will show you things to come.*" You may have heard people say, "I have a check in my spirit." What they are referring to is the Holy Spirit speaking to them. A check in your spirit is an uneasiness inside, a feeling that something is just not right. You may be watching or hearing something, and you feel an uneasiness, a cringe on the inside. This is the Holy Spirit leading you. The Holy Spirit, your alarm system, will let you know if something is wrong as your heart is open to His voice. We just need to pay attention to the Spirit of God and obey His voice. All of this comes by spending time with the Lord and yielding to Him. If you feel a check in your spirit or have a doubt about something, pray for the Lord's wisdom. Remember John 16:13 says the Holy Spirit will lead you into *all* truth. The Lord says, "*If any of you lack wisdom, let him ask of God, that giveth to all men liberally, and upbraideth not; and it shall be given him*" (James 1:5).

CHAPTER 2: GUARD YOUR HEART AND MIND

I am not trying to make you afraid but to give you wisdom to guard your life so that you can be victorious in your situation. When I lacked knowledge and had allowed ungodly stuff into my home, the Lord was faithful to show me so that I could clean my home. When I asked for forgiveness and stopped allowing in my home what He showed me was opening a door to the enemy, I saw improvement in my situation. Do not be afraid or feel condemned. Thank the Lord for His love and faithfulness to give you wisdom. James 1:5 says, "*If any of you lack wisdom, let him ask of God, that giveth to all men liberally, and upbraideth not; and it shall be given him.*" The Lord shows us these things to give us wisdom so that we can walk in the fullness of what He has for us. He wants us to walk in victory in life - not condemnation. The devil is the one who wants us to feel condemned, to paralyze us in our feelings, so we don't move on into the things that the Lord has for us.

You may say, "*I don't have control over the atmosphere of my home.*" Maybe you are married to a nonbeliever or live with those who don't believe as you do. First, pray and ask the Lord to put a hedge of protection around you, your heart and mind. Then ask the Lord to cleanse your heart and mind of the spiritual influences that have come in, and to give you wisdom on how to protect the atmosphere around you. Also, pray for those around you to be open to truth and for them to see the importance of protecting their own hearts and minds. If possible, sit down with them and share what is in your heart and what you would like to do or change in your life and surroundings. Pray for wisdom in the situation and guidance in your actions and words.

One day I was seeking the Lord for my own healing, He showed me that when I talked about or thought about my symptoms or how I felt, it would consume my thoughts. The more I thought about it, the worse I became. A lot of times my mind would wonder and begin thinking, "*What if this leads to something more serious?*" Soon I would find myself feeling afraid, and at times, having an overwhelming grip of fear. The Lord has had me overcome this fear by speaking His Word *strongly* and *fervently* to my mind and thoughts, playing teaching tapes on His Word while going to sleep, and filling my home continually with worship. There have been times that fear has tried to come into my mind again. I immediately remind myself what the Word says and the promises I have as a child of God.

There are also things that are considered Christian can bring fear. Once I read a couple of Christian novels about spiritual warfare and started listening to too many peoples' comments and negative stories that started a battle with fear. This demonstrates the importance of being careful of what you allow your eyes to see and your ears to hear. Not

CHAPTER 2: GUARD YOUR HEART AND MIND

all books, tapes, and movies that proclaim themselves to be Christian, are Godly. Listen to your spirit. Is your faith being strengthened? Are you being encouraged? If not, you do not need to read, listen to, or watch.

I heard it said once that most of the time FEAR is <u>F</u>alse <u>E</u>vidence <u>A</u>ppearing <u>R</u>eal. This really helped me put the fear that I was fighting into perspective. I began to realize what I was "fearing" was just in my thoughts. I was letting myself get to the point of consuming fear. I also realized that through the power of my Heavenly Father living inside me, I have the strength and ability to control what I let my mind think. That doesn't mean negative thoughts will not come and that it will be easy. Know that not all your thoughts come from yourself or God. They can come from others and/or Satan. But whatever thoughts come into your mind, if they are not in agreement with what God's Word says, you *have* the power, through the Lord living inside you, to replace your negative thoughts with what is right, God's Word. Interrupt your negative thoughts by *speaking* what the Word says. Ask God to show you when your thinking needs to be changed. The Word says,

> *"Finally, brethren, whatsoever things are true, whatsoever things are honest, whatsoever things are just, whatsoever things are pure, whatsoever things are lovely, whatsoever things are of good report; if*

YOU ARE HEALED OF THE LORD

there be any virtue, and if there be any praise, think on these things" (Philippians 4:8).

This is why we must guard our eyes and ears as much as possible from what we allow ourselves to listen to and see, whether it be movies, TV programs, commercials, websites, video games, music, books, or magazines. They can be filled with or have little subtle messages that are contrary to the Word of God, negative, or can cause us to doubt, fear, and have unbelief. Listen to your spirit. If you feel uneasy or agitated in your spirit (deep inside you) when you are participating in anything, pay attention to that. You may need to turn it off. Put it down. Walk away.

The Word also tells us *to take every thought captive to the obedience of Christ* (II Corinthians 10:5). What does it mean, "*to the obedience of Christ*"? John 1:1 says that, "*the Word was with God, the Word was God, and the Word became flesh and dwelt among us*"(John 1:14). What is the Word that became flesh and dwelt among us? Jesus, the Christ, was the Word. So, to be obedient to Christ is to be obedient to the Word of God, the Bible. We must cast down (kick out of our mind) imaginations and every high thing that exalts itself against the knowledge of Christ (against what the Word says).

You may ask, "*How do I remove something out of my mind?*" You start by telling yourself, "*No! I am not going*

CHAPTER 2: GUARD YOUR HEART AND MIND

to think about that or think that way." Then *make* yourself think other thoughts, such as what the Word says, the goodness of the Lord, the blessings you have in your life, being at your favorite place, or doing an activity you really enjoy. Remind yourself of the Lord's promises to you. Speak His Word out loud. When you speak out loud, your mind will listen to your words, and you can concentrate on that and not on the fear or negative thoughts that are trying to consume your mind.

Sometimes I battled fear the most was when I was trying to go to sleep. This is when all around you is quiet, and there are few other distractions. Knowing I needed to battle this with the Word of God, I would listen to teaching recordings or scriptures being read. I would make myself concentrate on what was being said. This would help me overcome fear and bring peaceful sleep.

When I first started doing this, fear did not leave instantaneous. It was a battle in my mind, but I was determined to win. With each passing night focusing on the Word, peace came quicker, and before long, I was able to go to sleep without the fear. I also noticed that the Word I was listening to would be spoken in my dreams and then come to mind throughout the day.

Fear is a feeling that can come with the thought that bad things are going to happen. Most of the time, we fear what we think <u>might</u> happen, not what is actually happening. It is a battle that starts in your mind. Many times

YOU ARE HEALED OF THE LORD

it is False Evidence Appearing Real. Yet, you may be in a very traumatic situation or receive news to be fearful of. No matter the situation, we must choose to believe and have faith in the report of the Lord (what the Word says). What does the report of the Lord say? It says He wants us healthy, strong, at peace, prosperous, and successful. The Word is the truth, and the truth will set you free (Psalm 119:43, 142, and 151; John 8:32). If a thought does not agree with the Word, then take it captive and cast it down. Make yourself push it out of your mind. Begin replacing the negative thought by speaking the Word of God. Fear may rise many times. Do not give up. Keep fighting it with the Word of the Lord. Victory will come.

What if you lack faith and struggle to believe? If you feel this way, try to spend as much time as you can reading the Word, speaking scriptures, speaking/praying His Word about your situation, listen to teachings of preachers of faith and the promises of His Word. Remember, *faith comes by hearing and hearing the Word of God* (Romans 10:17).

As you guard your heart and mind, speak what the Word says about yourself, your situation, or your healing, you will feel yourself becoming stronger and stronger in your mind and spirit, having hope, faith, and peace.

CHAPTER 3
THE SEED OF HIS WORD

AS YOU ARE SEEKING the Lord for your healing, He may only give you a specific word once about your healing. It can be His written or spoken Word. Mary, Jesus' mother, had only the one word from the Lord when the angel told her about giving birth to the Messiah. She had to explain it to others and live out God's will for her life on only that *one* word. That Word from God was a seed planted in her heart and spirit.

God wants to establish or plant Christ (the Word) in the hearts all of us. "*It is not I that liveth, but Christ that lives in me*" (Galatians 2:20). When we accept that seed of God's Word, that seed becomes planted in us, and it will grow and bring forth life (the fulfillment of that Word) as we feed, nurture, and protect it through prayer, reading the Word, and declaring the Word (speaking the Word).

Just like when a woman is pregnant, a *seed* is planted in her. The mother-to-be must feed and nurture the seed, the baby, by eating properly and taking care of herself. As she does this, the baby (seed) will grow and mature to completion. This is the same for our spiritual seed. We must feed and nurture the seed of the Word of God, so it will grow and mature

YOU ARE HEALED OF THE LORD

When a woman is pregnant, and the baby is growing, she will begin to change the things she does and says. She will begin to think more about everything in her life like what she eats, lifestyle, habits, and how these things will affect the baby. She will be very protective of that baby inside of her. Eventually, as the baby grows, she will begin to change the way she looks, the way she walks, and what she talks about. Everything will center on the baby. Everything she does will change. Same for the children of God. When we become "pregnant" with the Word and begin to nurture it, it will change the way we look, walk, and talk. *We will walk in newness of life* (Romans 6:4). *We will walk purposefully* (Romans 13:12-14). If the seed of the Word of God on the inside of us is not nurtured, it will begin to waste and die.

We must be careful of the seeds that we allow to be planted in us. What we allow ourselves to see and hear, who we hang out with, our conversations, what we watch and look upon, and what we read will plant seeds in our lives. We need to determine what kind of harvest we want and then be sure we are planting seeds for that kind of harvest.

How do you know if what you are hearing is good seed? First of all, does it line up or agree with God's Word or is it contrary to the Word? If you are still not sure, ask the Lord to show you if something is a good or bad seed. The more you spend time in the Word, the more

CHAPTER 3: THE SEED OF HIS WORD

knowledge and discernment you will have. It is better to try to do what is right and make a mistake than to not try at all. At times, you may mess up, miss the Lord's will, or make a mistake. Do not be in condemnation. Run to the arms of Jesus. He will get you back on track. This same principle applies to hearing the voice of God. How do you know if you are hearing His voice? One way to know is again ask yourself, "Does it agree with the Word of the Lord?" As we spend time in the Word and in prayer, we will become more and more in tune to His voice and less likely to miss His voice. He often speaks to His children in a still, small voice such as a thought that occurs to us or an inward conversation. Sometimes we receive a "sudden understanding" or just "know" the answer we have been seeking.

A way God confirmed this seed principle in my life was with my children. I am very careful of what I let my children watch on TV. I noticed that on a video they had, a boy was really sassy to others. It was even a Christian video. But I noticed the more they watched it, they started being sassy with me. We went on a TV fast as we did from time to time. With time away from that influence, they returned to their sweet selves. We are emotional beings that are affected by what is around us. That is why we need to be so careful of what seeds we are allowing to be planted in our lives.

YOU ARE HEALED OF THE LORD

You plant seeds in your life by what you speak. Proverbs 18:21 says that life and death are in the power of the tongue. Your tongue is a rudder. It steers your life. Where are your words leading you? Our words are a creative force or destructive force – good seed or bad seed. Psalms 34:13 says, "*Keep thy tongue from evil, and thy lips from speaking guile.*" Proverbs 15:23 says, "*A man hath joy by the answer of his mouth.*" "*There is that speaketh like the piercings of a sword: but the tongue of the wise is health*" (Proverbs 12:18). God's Word also says to *speak those things that are not as though they were* (Romans 4:17).

We must watch the words that we are speaking. Are our words good and positive, or are our words bad and negative? Speak words of faith and hope. Speaking the Word also helps build faith, so you are able to stand strong in knowing God is healing you. Speak the promises of God found in His Word and of good things. It builds up your faith and hope and encourages you.

Think about how you feel when you get around someone who is griping and complaining. Don't you start feeling down and depressed? Then think about when you get around someone who is happy and excited. Don't you feel yourself brightening up, your mood lifting? It's the same with the words that come out of our own mouth. That does not mean you never share with anyone what you are going through. We need each other's prayers. Remembering that "*One can put a thousand to*

CHAPTER 3: THE SEED OF HIS WORD

flight; two can send a legion fleeing" (Deuteronomy 32:30). The Word also says, "*Where two or three are gathered, there I am in the midst of them.*" (Matthew 18:20)

A simple example of how to share would be if you were having cold symptoms. Say to your praying friend, "I am fighting a cold," not "I have" a cold. Don't claim it as yours. Instead, ask, "Can you agree with me that this will go away, that every germ, bacteria, or virus will shrivel up and die?" If your friend asks you later how you are doing, and you are still fighting with the cold, don't just say I still have this cold. You could say something to the effect, "This cold is trying to be stubborn, but it has to go in the name of Jesus. I *am* the healed of the Lord."

You should also be selective on who you share and talk about your situation with. You want to ask people of faith, those who believe in healing and who will stand with you in faith believing, to pray for and with you. You don't want to share with those who will go around telling everyone your problems and saying, "Isn't that too bad." Be selective who you talk with about what you are going through. Ignore comments and distance yourself, if possible, from people who are speaking words of unbelief. Even when you are sharing with someone to ask them to pray, include God's promises, not just the details of the situation. "*Death and life are in the power of the tongue: and they that love it shall eat the fruit thereof.*"(Proverbs 18:21)

YOU ARE HEALED OF THE LORD

Also, you can plant seeds in other's lives for your own harvest. If you need healing, pray for those who are also in need of healing. It will take your mind off of yourself and plant seeds for your own harvest of healing. If you help take care of God's family's needs, He will take care of yours.

> Ephesians 6:8 says, *"Knowing that whatsoever good thing any man doeth, the same shall he receive of the Lord, whether he be bond or free."*
>
> Galatians 6:7-10 says, "*Be not deceived; God is not mocked: for whatsoever ye shall sow, that shall ye also reap. For he that soweth to his flesh shall of the flesh reap corruption; but he that soweth to the Spirit shall of the Spirit reap life everlasting. And let us not be weary in well doing: for in due season we shall reap, if we faint not. As we have therefore opportunity, let us do good unto all men, especially unto them who are of the household of faith.*"

Satan will try to make you doubt the Lord and His Word because he doesn't want people to trust God. People will also try to make you doubt God and His Word because of their own doubt and unbelief. They may say, "Well, if it is the Lord's will, He will heal you." Do not allow God's Word to be stolen from

CHAPTER 3: THE SEED OF HIS WORD

you. God's Word clearly tells us it is His will to heal. Jesus said that He came to do the will of the Father. What did Jesus do everywhere He went? He healed *all* who were sick and oppressed (Matthew 10:1, 12:12, Luke 4:40).

If you do not allow your worldly possessions to be stolen, then do not allow God's Word, your faith, hope, and courage to be stolen. You must learn to close your ears to Satan and to people without faith and say to yourself and others, "I do not believe or receive that. That is not what God's Word says and promises me. If God said it, then I believe it, and that settles it." Do not be afraid to stand up and fight for your healing. You could say to people, "I do not want to speak against what the Word of God says. I choose to believe the Word." The Lord will give you the words to say if the time comes for you to speak up. Just trust Him.

Do not stop praying and standing on the Word until you get an answer. Be persistent. Remember the lady in Luke 18 who kept going to the unjust judge until he gave her what she requested? If an unjust judge answers requests, how much more will your Heavenly Father give to you? God is a just Father and desires and longs to do good to you. You must set your mind or meditation on what you desire God to do. Find it in the Word, ask for it, write it down, and do not back away from it or let anybody or anything talk you out of it.

YOU ARE HEALED OF THE LORD

Don't give up. Keep fighting and standing on the Word of the Lord.

Imagine if you wanted to protect your house from someone just walking in. You would lock the door. What if you wanted to protect your home from a thief who wanted to steal from you, kill you and your family, and destroy your home? You would lock the doors and windows, put lights up all around your home, put in an alarm system and a wall up all around your property with barbed wire, lights, and alarms.

Satan is like that thief that "*cometh not, but for to steal, to kill, and destroy*" (John 10:10). We must keep our defenses up in every area. Our defenses are kept up by spending time in God's presence, through praising and worshiping Him, prayer, reading and studying the Word, praying the Word, keeping you and your family covered daily with prayer, and pleading the blood of Jesus over your life every day. Then we allow the Lord to fight for us. The Lord is our rock, defense, and strong high tower. *The battle is not yours, but mine, says the Lord* (2 Chronicles 20:15). Do this in faith and not fear.

But you may say, "Well I am afraid and do fear." Do not condemn yourself. Most of us start out in fear. Then, start doing it afraid. Face your fear with the Word. The more you spend time with the Lord in prayer and reading His Word, the faster fear will leave, and faith is strengthened. Fear cannot live where faith abides.

CHAPTER 3: THE SEED OF HIS WORD

You may be thinking, "*When I was in the world, I was never sick like this or had these kinds of problems.*" Don't blame God for your problems or illnesses. He is not the source of sickness and disease; Satan is. We are in a war against Satan. When you were in the world, you were already on Satan's side. Your eyes were blind to the truth of the Word and the goodness and promises of God. Praise God, we know how it all ends. Who wins the war? The Lord does.

When you get saved, you become Satan's enemy. Your heart is now open to truth. You are a light in the darkness that Satan wants to put out. When you become a child of God and you get a headache, Satan will try to lie to you to make you think it's a tumor, maybe a cancerous tumor. The Word says that Satan is the father of lies. The thoughts he tries to give us will always be lies and against the Word of God. Do not bite his hook of fear. You need to immediately cast down those thoughts. The Word says to "*cast down imaginations and every high thing that exalts itself against the knowledge of God*" (II Corinthians 10:5). What is the knowledge of God? It is what the Bible says. Immediately say, "Satan, you are a liar. I do not accept your lies. The Word says that I am the healed of the Lord. I walk in divine health." Say whatever else the Lord puts in your heart to say. Use the Word.

When Jesus was tempted in the wilderness, (yes, even Jesus, the very Son of God, was tempted), what did He do? Jesus said, "*It is written!*" (Matthew 4:1-11). Whatever Satan would say to Jesus, Jesus always responded with what was written in the Word of God. He didn't fight battles in His own human ability. Jesus spoke what the Word said.

That is why we too must learn the Word, so we can speak it. You may say, "*I already bit that hook of fear.*" Then stop right where you are at this moment and say, "*Lord, I am sorry for not believing You and following fear. I confess right now that You are my healer and deliverer. Satan, you are a liar. I will not accept your lies any longer. I will believe what the Word says. In Jesus name, I am the healed of the Lord. I will see my Heavenly Father's promises come to pass in my life.*"

Satan tries to attack us, distract us, and pull us away from God and His promises. Satan doesn't want you to grow closer to the Lord for he knows that it makes you more powerful, and that scares him. When you are covered with the presence of God from spending so much time with Him, Satan will cringe at your very presence because what he sees is the presence of the Lord. Do not fear. The Word tells us over and over again not to fear. "*The battle is not yours, but God's*", (2 Chronicles 20:15). The Lord fights for us as we trust and rely on Him. We do our part, loving on the Lord through praise and worship, spending time in His precious Word, praying,

CHAPTER 3: THE SEED OF HIS WORD

seeking His face, being watchful of the seeds we allow to be planted in our hearts, and being obedient to His voice and Word, then we can rest in Him and let Him take care of His part. Just like you would take care of and fight to protect your own child or those you love, God will take care of us even more as we look to Him. His strength is our strength.

Once we are healed and delivered, we have promises in the Word that sickness shall not return. Nahum 1:9 says, "*What do ye imagine against the Lord? He will make an utter end? Affliction shall not rise up the second time.*" Romans 8:15 says, "*For ye have not received the spirit of bondage again to fear; but ye have received the Spirit of adoption, whereby we cry, Abba, Father.*"

Galatians 5:1 also says, "*Stand fast therefore in the liberty wherewith Christ hath made us free, and be not entangled again with the yoke of bondage.*"

Stand firm, and hold strong to His promises, planting good seed in your life and the lives of others!

CHAPTER 4

YOUR RIGHTS AND PRIVILEGES AS A CHILD OF GOD

YOU HAVE SPECIAL RIGHTS and privileges as a child of God. You ask, "*How can you say that we are the children of God?*" Look at Galatians 4:4-7,

> "*But when the fullness of the time was come, God sent forth His Son, made of a woman, made under the law, to redeem them that were under the law, that <u>we might receive the adoption of sons</u>. And because <u>ye are sons</u>, God hath sent forth the Spirit of His Son into your hearts, crying, Abba, Father. Wherefore thou art no more a servant, but <u>a son</u>; and if a son, then <u>an heir of God through Christ</u>.*"

II Corinthians 6:16-18 says,

> "*As God hath said, I will dwell in them, and walk in them, and I will be their God, and they shall be my people. Wherefore come out from among them, and be ye separate, saith the Lord, and touch not*

YOU ARE HEALED OF THE LORD

the unclean thing; and I will receive you, and will be <u>a Father unto you, and ye shall be my sons and daughters</u>, saith the Lord Almighty."

So, if Jesus is the Lord of your life, then you are a child of God and a part of His family. As a child of God, you have the right to use your family name, the name of Jesus.

What are some of those rights? The Word says that *everything in heaven and earth and under the earth that is named must bow its knee to the name of Christ Jesus* (Philippians 2:10). So if I have the authority of the name of Jesus, because I am a child of God, then everything I speak to in His name must bow to His name. That is why we pray in Jesus name. John 14:14 says that *if we ask anything in the name of Jesus, it shall be given to us.* Many people take that scripture by itself and think that it means they can ask for anything, and they will get it. We must also keep in mind that the Word says *if we ask according to His will, He hears us* (I John 5:14). How do we know if it is His will? The Bible tells us most things that are God's will. From God's Word, we know that it is His will to heal us. So, then we can know that if we are asking for healing, God will give it to us.

Jesus' name is above every *name.* Jesus' name is above the name of depression. It is above the name of cancer. Everything that has a name must bow its knee to

CHAPTER 4: YOUR RIGHTS AND PRIVILEGES

the name of JESUS. Hallelujah! Isn't that good news?! And it is all available to you because you are a child of God. That is why when we pray for something, we say, *"In the name of Jesus."*

If the Word does not say specifically if something is His will, ask the Lord if it is. One of the scriptures I pray when I need the Lord's wisdom is Ephesians 1:17-23.

> *"That the God of our Lord Jesus Christ, the Father of glory, may give unto you the spirit of wisdom and revelation in the knowledge of him: The eyes of your understanding being enlightened; that ye may know what is the hope of his calling, and what the riches of the glory of his inheritance in the saints, And what is the exceeding greatness of his power to us-ward who believe, according to the working of his mighty power, Which he wrought in Christ, when he raised him from the dead, and set him at his own right hand in the Heavenly places, Far above all principality, and power, and might, and dominion, and every name that is named, not only in this world, but also in that which is to come: And hath put all things under his feet, and gave him to be the head over all things to the church, Which is his body, the fullness of him that filleth all in all."*

YOU ARE HEALED OF THE LORD

In this scripture, do you also see the power that was given to Christ? He was set at God's own right hand far above *all* principality, and power, and might, and dominion, and every name that is named, not only in this world, but also in that which is to come.

Another right as a child of God is the power of His Word. The Lord is faithful to His Word. Psalms 138:2 says *He puts His Word above His name.* And if you look up all the scriptures regarding the name of the Lord, you will see how *powerful* His name is. (Refer to the "Power and Authority of God and His Word" scripture list in Chapter 10.) So if He puts His Word above His name, and His name is above every name, then you can rely on the Word to *never fail. His Word does not go up to Him void, but it shall accomplish that which I please, and it shall prosper in the thing where to I sent it.* (Isaiah 55:11).

The Lord also says to put *Him in remembrance of His Word* (Isaiah 43:26). We remind God of His word, not because He forgets, but it is to remind ourselves of His promises and to build our faith. As we speak His Word, we are hearing it. *Faith comes by hearing and hearing the Word* (Romans 10:17). *He will always perform what His Word says* (Isaiah 55:11).

As a child of God, you also have the power of the blood of Jesus. The blood of Jesus is your wall or hedge of protection. *The life of anything is in its blood* (Leviticus 17:11). When we pray and plead the blood of Jesus over

CHAPTER 4: YOUR RIGHTS AND PRIVILEGES

something, we are praying the very power of the life of Jesus over it. Everything that Jesus' shedding His blood did for us on the cross at Calvary is available to us as we "plead the blood of Jesus".

In the Old Testament, the blood of the lamb was what God used to protect the children of Israel from the death that was coming to Egypt. Let's read it.

> *"They shall take to them every man a lamb, a lamb for a house. Your lamb shall be without blemish. Israel shall kill it in the evening. And they shall take of the blood, and strike it on the two side posts and on the upper doorpost of the house. And the blood shall be to you for a token upon the houses where ye are: and when I see the blood, I will pass over you, and the plague shall not be upon you to destroy you, when I smite the land of Egypt. For the Lord will pass through to smite the Egyptians; and when he seeth the blood upon the lintel, and on the two side posts, the Lord will pass over the door, and will not suffer the destroyer to come in unto your houses to smite you."* (Exodus 12: 3, 5, 6-7, 13, 23)

God had them do this for their protection and to point us to Jesus and what His blood would do for us. That Jesus was to be the final, perfect, spotless lamb that was slain for us.

YOU ARE HEALED OF THE LORD

How do we know Jesus is that Lamb of God? John the Baptist said of Jesus when he saw Him coming, "*Behold the Lamb of God, which taketh away the sin of the world.*" Revelation 13:8 tells us that *Jesus was the Lamb slain from the foundation of the world.* I Peter 1:18-19 says, "*Forasmuch as ye know that ye were not redeemed with corruptible things, as silver and gold, from your vain conversation received by tradition from your fathers; but with the precious blood of Christ, as a lamb without blemish and without spot: who verily was foreordained before the foundation of the world, but was manifest in these last times for you.*" At the last supper Jesus had with His disciples, He took bread, broke it, and said, "*Take, eat, this is my body which is broken for you.*" He took a cup and said, "*This cup is the new testament in my blood: this do ye, as oft as ye drink it, in remembrance of me*" (Luke 22:20). Revelation 12:11 says, "*They overcame by the blood of the Lamb and the word of our testimony.*" Praise God, the Lord has *redeemed us by His blood* to give us a new life. (Ephesians 1:7)

There is power in the blood of Jesus to save us and deliver us. Since Jesus is *our* lamb slain for us, we are to use His blood in our lives. Just as the Israelites applied the blood of the lamb to the doors of their homes, we apply the blood of the lamb to the doors of our lives by praying and saying, "*I plead the blood of Jesus over _____.*" Fill in the blank with whatever area of your life you need covered: your body, mind, family, or situation. The list is

CHAPTER 4: YOUR RIGHTS AND PRIVILEGES

endless. There is an old hymn that says, *"There is power, power, wonder working power in the blood of the Lamb. There is power, power, wonder working power in the precious blood of the Lamb."* It is a great song to sing and remind us of the power of the blood of Jesus available for our lives.

Another benefit is to anoint with oil. To anoint with oil, simply means to put oil on your hand and apply it to the person or item. In the Bible when something is anointed, it is consecrated and set apart for a special use or purpose. In Exodus 29 and 30, the Lord commanded the priests to anoint with oil the tabernacle and the items in it. When we anoint with oil, we are saying that this particular item or person is being consecrated and set apart for the Lord.

In the New Testament, Jesus also told us to anoint those who are sick and pray for them.

> *"Is any among you sick? Let him call for the elders of the church; and let them pray over him, anointing him with oil in the name of the Lord; and the prayer of faith shall save him that is sick, and the Lord shall raise him up" (James 5:14-15).*

When we anoint the sick with oil, we are saying, "This person is now set apart for the Lord to work in their lives according to His Word and will for their lives."

YOU ARE HEALED OF THE LORD

You may say, "I am not a pastor, priest or elder. How do I have authority to anoint someone or something with oil?" As a child of God, He made you to be kings and priests in your life. Revelation 1:6 says, *"And hath made us kings and priests unto God and his Father; to him be glory and dominion for ever and ever. Amen."* As a child of God, He has made you a *priest* with the rights, privileges, authority of and use of the name of Jesus, the power of His blood, and to anoint with oil consecrating and declaring someone or something is set apart for the Lord's use and purpose.

In the Bible, they used olive oil and other special spice oils like myrrh, sweet cinnamon, calamus, and cassia. You do not have to possess these oils specifically for anointing. Use whichever oil you have at the time you need it. I pray over whatever oil I have before I use it and ask the Lord to sanctify and purify the oil for His use. As we anoint with oil to mark something as the Lord's and out of obedience to the Word, the Lord is faithful to perform His Word.

So, when we accept Jesus as our Lord, we are made a part of God's family and given the right to use that family name, plead the blood, and partake of all the benefits of being a part of His family. Psalms 103: 2 tells us to "*forget not all His benefits.*"

If you have not made Jesus Lord of your life to become a child of God so that all these things are

CHAPTER 4: YOUR RIGHTS AND PRIVILEGES

available to you, let's pray right now and make Jesus Lord of your life.

Father, I come to you in the name of Jesus. I repent and ask for forgiveness of all my sins. I need you. I give my life to you. Right now, I make Jesus Lord of my life. I know and believe that Jesus is the Son of God and that He died on the cross for me and was raised from the dead so that I may have eternal life. I accept what Jesus did on the cross for me. And I choose to live for Jesus. I thank you Father God for forgiving me and making me your child. In Jesus name, Amen.

It is that simple. Now you can partake of what the Word says is available to you with confidence, knowing you are a child of God. You have been adopted into His family. *Old things are passed away. Behold, all things are made new* (II Corinthians 5:17). You now have the full rights and privileges promised us as a member of God's family.

CHAPTER 5

SOME REASONS PEOPLE MAY NOT BE RECEIVING HEALING

YOU MAY BE DOING all you know to do, but you are not seeing your healing come forth. There may be something in your life that could be keeping you from receiving your healing. There are some reasons you may not be receiving your healing:

- Unforgiveness
- Bitterness
- Strife
- Murmuring and complaining
- Speaking against God's anointed or His anointing
- Disobedience to God and His Word/out of God's will for your life
- Lack of knowledge of God's Word
- Too busy/stressful life

YOU ARE HEALED OF THE LORD

- No vision for the future
- Your own thoughts and meditation
- Lifestyle and/or habits
- Strongholds

Unforgiveness

Unforgiveness is hard on your emotions and on your body. When you walk around angry, sad, and upset, how do you feel? Your mind and body feel awful. You may feel tense, nervous, jittery, shaky, have headaches, stomachaches, etc. When you are tense and upset, your body releases adrenaline. Even a low level of adrenaline for long periods of time will start to break down your body. This alone can cause physical problems in your body.

Not only is unforgiveness hard on our bodies, the Lord commands us to forgive. Ephesians 4:32 says, *"And be ye kind one to another, tenderhearted, FORGIVING one another, even as God for Christ's sake hath forgiven you."* Colossians 3:13 says, *"Forbearing one another, and FORGIVING one another, if a man has a quarrel against any: even as Christ forgave you, so also do ye."* Luke 6:37 also says, *"Judge not and ye shall not be judged: condemn not, and ye shall not be condemned: FORGIVE and ye shall be FORGIVEN."*

Do you sometimes feel that your prayers are not getting to the ears of God? Mark 11:25-26 says, *"And when*

CHAPTER 5: NOT RECEIVING HEALING

ye stand praying, forgive, if ye have aught against any: that your Father also which is in heaven may forgive you your trespasses. But if ye do not forgive, neither will your Father which is in heaven forgive your trespasses." Check your life and make sure you do not have unforgiveness separating you from the Father. If you do, the first step is to ask the Lord for forgiveness for being unforgiving. Then you must forgive.

You may ask, "*How do I forgive when I have been hurt so badly or done so wrong?*" First, you ask the Lord to help you. Then you forgive by your will or choice. You say, "*I choose by my will to forgive* _____ (you fill in the blank) *through the power of Jesus name. I choose to release them of this wrong. I will walk in love toward them for I have forgiven them.*"

You may not feel a change right away. It may take some time. You may have to profess your forgiveness many times, but soon you will begin to notice a difference when you see that person or think of them as you continue to pray for them and your own heart toward them. Every time you think of that person or see them and the feelings of hurt and unforgiveness rise up, keep telling yourself, "*I forgave them by my will and choice. Now body and mind, you line up, come into agreement with that forgiveness, in Jesus name.*" As you trust the Lord, He will help you and heal your heart. Before too long, you will notice that your body and mind have lined up with that choice of forgiveness. Remember that forgiveness of others does not mean that you agree with or like what they did, but it does mean that what they did no longer has power over you.

Bitterness

Bitterness is the next phase in lingering unforgiveness. If you harbor unforgiveness, it will turn into bitterness. Bitterness carries over into other areas of your life and toward people who have not offended you. You may become easily angry - and every little thing sets you off. Bitterness becomes the "glasses" through which you see and filter your personal interactions. You start to expect the worst in others when you are walking in bitterness. Ask the Lord to show you the root cause of your bitterness if you do not know. If we seem to be in conflict with others a lot, ask the Lord to show you why. Ask the Lord for forgiveness and then forgive others by your will and choice.

Strife

A lot of times, strife is the result of unforgiveness and bitterness. These three can go hand in hand. If it is because we are holding unforgiveness, ask the Lord for forgiveness and then forgive others by your will and choice. Strife can also be caused by others' actions or words, causing hurt feelings. Say to yourself, "*They are troubled today. I will not*

CHAPTER 5: NOT RECEIVING HEALING

let the actions of others dictate what kind of day I will have." I know this is easier said than done. The more you practice not taking things personally and try to understand why others are doing what they do, the easier it will be to not be offended and to stop strife in its tracks.

We never know what others have faced or are facing in their lives or why they may be acting or reacting the way they are. It is important to have compassion for others and to try to see into their heart. *A soft answer and an understanding response a lot of times turns away wrath* (Proverbs 15:1). Choose to think good of others and understand them first.

We must also check and see if we are spending time with and befriending strifeful people. Proverbs 22:24-26 says, *"Make no friendship with an angry man; and with a furious man thou shalt not go: Lest thou learn his ways, and get a snare to thy soul. Be not thou one of them that strike hands, or of them that are sureties for debts."* What we fill our minds with will affect us. Unless directed by the Lord, our companions should not be people of strife. If you have no choice in the matter, keep this area covered in prayer. James 3:16 says, *"For where envying and strife is, there is confusion and every evil work."* Romans 13:13-14 says, *"Let us walk honestly, as in the day; not in rioting and drunkenness, not in chambering and wantonness, not in strife and envying. But put ye on the Lord Jesus Christ, and make no provision for the flesh, to fulfill the lusts thereof."*

YOU ARE HEALED OF THE LORD

Strife affects you physically, mentally, and spiritually. Check your life to see if strife is a part of it. Try to overcome being strifeful by choosing to be positive! It does not always come by circumstance. Many times in life, things happen that can easily steal our joy. We have to choose how we respond. Proverbs 15:23 say, "*Joy comes by the answer of our mouth.*" Give this area to the Lord in prayer. The Lord will help you.

Murmuring and Complaining

If we are inflexible, stubborn, murmur, complain, or act as though everything has to be perfect or we are not happy, we are being unthankful and ungrateful for what we have and where we are. When we are in an ungrateful state of mind, every word we speak is like a fire set to consume our joy and hope.

Know that a weapon of victory is your words. Murmuring and complaining separates you from God and stops His hand from moving in your life. Remember what happened to the children of Israel after God had brought them out of Egypt and its bondages? They murmured and complained continually.

> Numbers 11:1 says, "*And when the people complained, it displeased the Lord: and the Lord heard it; and his anger was kindled; and the fire of the Lord*

CHAPTER 5: NOT RECEIVING HEALING

burnt among them, and consumed them that were in the uttermost parts of the camp."

Because of complaining, they had to wonder in the wilderness for forty years until the older generation had passed away. Then the new generation was able to enter the Promised Land. The older generation dying is a picture of our old man or nature needing to die and our new man or nature in Christ being able to enter and receive the promises of God. We do not want to miss our Promised Land or fulfillment of God's promises to us because we will not stop murmuring and complaining. We have so much to be thankful for. Just think, even if the Lord never did a thing for us during our walk with Him here on this earth, He gave us salvation through the death of His Dear Son. That in itself is enough for us to be thankful for our entire life here on earth. We get to go to heaven and live with our Heavenly Father for eternity.

Life and death are in the power of the tongue (Proverbs 18:21). *The mouth of a righteous man is a well of life* (Proverbs 10:11). When we speak righteous words, they bring life. Are you speaking words that are bringing life and victory and are in agreement with the Word of God? You feed your heart and mind by the words you speak. What you speak goes into your ears and then into your mind, which feeds your heart. We can change a lot of things in our lives by what we speak and by remembering life and death are in the power of your tongue. As Proverbs 15:23 says, "*Your joy comes by the answer of our mouth.* Philemon 1:6 says, "*That the communication of thy faith may become effectual by the acknowledging of every good thing which is in you in Christ Jesus.*"

Speaking against God's Anointed and His Anointing

Romans 13:1-2 says, "*Let every soul be subject unto the higher powers. For there is no power but of God: the powers that be are ordained of God. Whosoever therefore resisteth the power, resisteth the ordinance of God: and they that resist shall receive to themselves damnation.*"

David is a good example to follow when talking about how to deal with God's anointed servants. I Samuel 26:9 says, "*David's heart smote him, because he had cut off Saul's skirt. And he said unto his men; The Lord forbid that I should do this thing unto my master, the Lord's anointed, to stretch forth mine hand against him, seeing he is the anointed of the Lord.*" David also said in I Samuel 26:9, "*For who can stretch forth his hand against the Lord's anointed, and be guiltless?*" How can David say that Saul was the Lord's anointed? At this time, Saul was wicked. He was on a manhunt to kill David, who once lived in Saul's house as one of his sons. Yet God had picked Saul

CHAPTER 5: NOT RECEIVING HEALING

and anointed him king. The whole story can be found in I Samuel chapter 10.

The first chapter of II Samuel gives the account of how David responded to Saul's death, "*Then David took hold on his clothes, and rent them; and likewise all the men that were with him. And they mourned, and wept, and fasted until evening, for Saul, and for Jonathan his son.*" And David said unto him who killed Saul, "*How wast thou not afraid to stretch forth thine hand to destroy the Lord's anointed? And David lamented with this lamentation over Saul and over Jonathan his son.*" David stated in I Samuel 26:23, "*The Lord render to every man his righteousness and his faithfulness: for the Lord delivered thee into my hand today, but I would not stretch forth mine hand against the Lord's anointed.*"

God called David His beloved. This account shows us David's heart and that we need to be careful of how we treat those in leadership positions. We may not agree with what they say or do, but they still need to be treated with respect. They are people, and people make mistakes. This is why it is so vitally important that we keep *all* those in leadership covered in prayer. I Timothy 2:1-3 says, "*I exhort therefore, that, first of all, supplications, prayers, intercessions, and giving of thanks, be made for all men; For kings, and for all that are in authority; that we may lead a quiet and peaceable life in all godliness and honesty. For this is good and acceptable in the sight of God our Savior.*"

YOU ARE HEALED OF THE LORD

It is easy to see and criticize others, but what if you were in their position? In a Godly manner, let the voice of the righteous and righteousness be heard. This does not mean to be obedient or follow our leaders if what they ask you to do is immoral, unrighteous, or against the Word of the Lord. This is why it is also vitally important for us to pray for our pastors and for direction on who to vote for. Not only do we keep our government leaders in prayer, but also our spiritual leaders

Disobedience to God and His Word/Out of God's Will for Your Life

Deuteronomy 28:58-62 says, *"If thou wilt not observe to do all the words of this law that are written in this book, that thou mayest fear this glorious and fearful name, The Lord thy God; Then the Lord will make thy plagues wonderful, and the plagues of thy seed, even great plagues, and of long continuance, and sore sicknesses, and of long continuance. Moreover, he will bring upon thee all the diseases of Egypt, which thou wast afraid of; and they shall cleave unto thee. Also every sickness, and every plague, which is not written in the book of this law, them will the Lord bring upon thee, until thou be destroyed. And ye shall be left few in number whereas ye were as the stars of heaven for multitude; because thou wouldest not obey the voice of the Lord thy God."*

CHAPTER 5: NOT RECEIVING HEALING

So you see, sickness can be from disobedience to God, out of His will and out from under His covering. You need to seek the Lord to see if your sickness is from not having something right in your life. Are you being obedient to the Lord and His commands?

I do not believe because you fail, sin, or do something wrong that it is all over for your healing, and you are not worthy of God's love and His healing. I used to think that. When I first started seeking God for my healing. I would be progressing well in my faith and my walk with the Lord, studying the Word, getting it deep into my heart, really starting to believe for my healing. Then all of the sudden, my husband and I would get into an argument, and I would say some unkind things. Afterwards, I felt awful. I felt hopeless and defeated, that I had blown it. I was sure God was upset with me. I felt I was not even worthy of His love now, let alone His healing power. This is a lie of Satan. Satan wants you to believe this so you will give up.

We are made righteous by the blood of Jesus. If we could be worthy of God's love all by ourselves, then why did Jesus come and die for us? *He died for us while we were yet sinners* (Romans 5:8). Christ died for us because He knew that we could never be worthy of anything from God in our own ability. He created us. He knows us. He knows that we are sinful by nature (in the flesh) because

YOU ARE HEALED OF THE LORD

of the sin that Adam and Eve allowed into the human race. When you sin, ask God for forgiveness. Now this does not mean that you keep on doing wrong and say God will forgive me. That would be willful sinning, and we are foolishly testing God. It says in Matthew 4:7 "*Do not tempt the Lord your God.*" But if we do "mess up" while we are trying to be obedient to God's Word, God is waiting with open arms to forgive us, cleanse us, and bring us back into right relationship with Him (Romans chapters 6-8). Even if you have been willfully sinning and you make a choice to get things right in your life, God is there with open arms ready to take you in.

If you have children who try to be good and obedient but they happen to make bad choices, you are there with open arms to forgive and love them back to where they should be. But if you have a child who is always testing you, testing the rules, and who doesn't seem to care about obedience, your grace and favor for them runs out, and they miss out on the blessings they could be receiving from you. They are moving out from your covering. But if that rebellious child sees their wrong, repents, and wants to do right, you are there waiting with open arms, excited to have that relationship restored. The story of the prodigal son found in Luke 15:11-32 is good to read. It can help you see and understand the way God looks at us.

CHAPTER 5: NOT RECEIVING HEALING

If you slip or make a mistake, then repent, set your mind again, and keep going. No matter how many times you may mess up, get up, and keep going. You must be tenacious, determined to receive the promises of God. Never give up until you receive! If you find yourself giving up, refocus, and go again. DO NOT give up! KEEP GOING!

Lack of Knowledge of God's Word

Hosea 4:6 says, "*My people are destroyed for lack of knowledge.*" When we lack knowledge of what the Word of God says, we don't know what God has promised us and what is available to us as His children.

The Word also says to cast down imaginations and every high thing that exalts itself *against the knowledge of God.* A good way to search the Bible for what the Word says, so you know what thoughts are not from God and what imaginations to cast down, is to use a Bible concordance or app, or search online resources. Look up scriptures regarding what you are unsure about. God will reveal the truth to you.

Think of it this way. Let's say that you want to make banana bread. You don't know how to make it. You have ten cookbooks in the cabinet, but you have never opened them to look to see if there is a recipe for banana bread. You keep walking past your bananas and saying, "*I have all these bananas going to waste. It sure would be great to make bread with them."* It just so happens that one of your cookbooks is all about different kinds of banana bread, but you never open it. You pass the bananas day after day and watch them rot. *"Too bad I didn't know how to make banana bread,"* you say as you throw away the bananas. Yet the answer had been there the whole time. A simple example, but this is what we are doing when we don't read the Bible for answers to what's going on in our lives. The answers are right there in His Word. But if we never open it to find out, how will we know. *Look, seek, and find!*

Too Busy/Stressful Life

We can be sick because we have too much going on in our lives; we're too busy. In our society today, we are expected to *"keep up with the Jones,"* to be involved with everything, and to keep up appearances. This is not God's will. He only expects us to do what He has called us to do. We may be involved in many activities. They all may be good and Godly, but not God's will for your life. I encourage you to pray before you accept many commitments. If something is not God's will for your life, do not be afraid to say no.

Being too busy is taxing on the body and can begin to wear you down physically, mentally, and spiritually, causing

CHAPTER 5: NOT RECEIVING HEALING

stress. When your body is overloaded, your immune system becomes taxed as well as your muscles, joints, nerve endings, etc. This can lead to sickness. So, make sure your life is manageable. Do not be afraid of eliminating some activities from your life. Do not worry what people will think. God does not want us to worry about being men pleasers but to focus on following His leading. God says that "*His burden is easy and His yoke is light.* (Matthew 11:30)"

If we know that what we are doing is God's will for our life and we are still feeling extremely pressured, then we are probably not relying on God to help us do these things. We are more than likely trying to do them in our own power. Are we looking to Him for help, or are we trying to do it all by ourselves?

For some, saying no to people can be very hard to do. I was raised not to offend people, which is a good thing, and this principle was deeply ingrained in me. I got it out of perspective, though. I was always worried that if I told people no when I had the ability and/or time to do what I was asked, I would offend them. I would be tormented with the thought that I was offending someone. Even if I had a real reason I could not do something, I was very concerned I would hurt their feelings. The Lord had to bring balance into my life in this area.

The Bible does say *we are to be careful of offense* (Matthew 18:6-7). This means we do not react and treat people without thinking about their feelings. We can say things in a nice way, even no, such as, "*I would love to, but I can't right now,*" or "*I would love to, but God has been dealing with me on not taking on too much, so I can't do that right now.*" Say whatever the Lord lays on your heart to say.

I still struggle with this occasionally. Every so often when people ask me to do things, my first response is to say yes if I know I have the ability. But I have to stop myself and see if this something I should do.

No Vision for the Future

As the Word says, "*Without a vision my people parish*" (Proverbs 29:18). Some may say, "*Why have a vision for the future? You see the signs of the times that Jesus is coming soon. The work will never be finished.*" But we need vision for our own well-being, something to live for and strive for daily. The Lord said to "*occupy till I come*" (Luke 19:13). This is for our own self-worth, self-esteem, confidence, hope, and, yes, health.

If you lack a vision or dream, something to work toward, then pray and ask the Lord to give you a vision for your future. He may have already given you a vision, but that vision has died. Ask the Lord to renew that vision.

The Lord has something for everyone to do. Some callings are small, and some are big. No matter the call,

CHAPTER 5: NOT RECEIVING HEALING

He wants us all to be faithful and work at whatever we put our hand to as we do it for Him. You may be a housekeeper, a mail carrier, a lawyer, a doctor, a janitor, a student, a stay-at-home mom, a dad, a grandparent... the list can go on and on. Your vision could be to just pray for your family and friends and to be an encouragement. Be faithful wherever you are and to whatever you are called to do. Do everything as you would do it for the Lord.

Your Own Thoughts or Meditation

Your own thoughts can make you physically sick. Psalms 102:4-5 gives us an example of David being so overcome in his mind that it made him sick. David said, *"My heart is smitten, and withered like grass; so that I forget to eat my bread. By reason of the voice of my groaning my bones cleave to my skin."*

The majority of your battles happen in your mind. This is where Satan attacks you first. Thoughts will come into your mind. You must pay attention. Is what you are thinking about coming from God, pleasing to God, and what we should be thinking about? You can tell this by whether or not it is in agreement with the Word of God and by asking yourself, "Does it bring hope, peace, and comfort?" Philippians 4:8 says, *"Finally, brethren, whatsoever things are true, whatsoever things are honest, whatsoever things are just, whatsoever things are pure, whatsoever things are lovely, whatsoever things are of good report; if there be any virtue, and if there be any praise, think on these things."*

The Word also says, *"By the stripes of Jesus, we were healed."* (I Peter 2:24) Do your thoughts line up with this? Remember, *"For though we walk in the flesh, we do not war after the flesh. For the weapons of our warfare are not carnal, but mighty through God to the pulling down of strong holds; casting down imaginations, and every high thing that exalteth itself against the knowledge of God, and bringing into captivity every thought to the obedience of Christ."* (II Corinthians 10:3-5) You must cast down imaginations. You do this by speaking to yourself what the Word of God says. Say to yourself, *"That is not my thought. I will not think on that. The Lord says _____."* Then speak what the Word of God says. Tell yourself what you will think on. Remind yourself if God said it, that settles it. *Make yourself* think about what the Lord says in His Word about your situation by interrupting the thought and immediately replacing it with His Word regarding the situation. The more you do this, the sooner faith, hope, and joy comes. Before long, it will be a habit.

If you are not sure what His Word says about something, search the Bible to find it. Start looking up scriptures that pertain to your situation, study them, write them down, and memorize them. A couple of things I have done is write them on 3x5 cards that I put on

CHAPTER 5: NOT RECEIVING HEALING

my bathroom mirror, refrigerator, and my office desk. I would also keep a stack with me to pull out and read whenever needed. You could also put them in the Notes app. of your phone or computer, or highlight them on your Bible app. Ask the Lord to help you find the scriptures. I have also tried to help you find these scriptures. The last half of the book is for this purpose.

As you search and study the Word of God, it becomes a light that enters into our hearts and brings light (Psalms 119:130). Light brings hope and an uplifting of our spirit. Then we become the light to this world. *We become like a bright well lite city on a hill which cannot be hid* (Matthew 5:14). Think about when you have been in a dark, cool building for a while. You feel chilled. You walk outside, and the sun is warm and bright. Inside yourself, you go, A*ahh!* You stand and bask in the sun. It feels so good to you. You feel uplifted, and a joy rises up inside you. This is the same feeling when the light of God's Word enters the dark cold parts of your life.

Picture a heart. Picture it filled with the Word, I mean filled up, no space left. When Satan throws his fiery darts at it, the dart hits that heart so full of the Word it bounces back as if it had hit a brick wall. Now picture a heart that is not filled up all the way with the Word of God. There are open places. So, when Satan throws his darts at it, the dart doesn't bounce back. It is able to penetrate and cause harm. We need to stay filled up with the Word.

How do you fill up with the Word? We can do this by meditating on it. I do not mean the world's picture of meditating, sitting on the floor with your legs crossed and humming. We meditate on the Word by constantly reading, studying, and listening to it, saying it out loud and to ourselves over and over, memorizing, singing, and thinking about it. Listen to teachings about the Word. Listen to music that contains the Word. Watch videos of ministers teaching the Word. Do this while you are doing your daily activities, driving your car, at work, exercising, cleaning, mowing the lawn, etc. This needs to be as much as possible (continual), not just once a day, once a week, or even just one time.

The Word is full of power. Hebrews 4:12 says, "*For the Word of God is quick, and powerful, and sharper than a two-edged sword, piercing even to the dividing asunder of soul and spirit, and of the joints and marrow, and is a discerner of the thought and intents of the heart.*" Satan cannot stand up against the Word of God. Remember, when Satan tempted Jesus in the wilderness, Jesus always answered with, "*It is written... It is written...*" (Luke 4). Jesus spoke the Word of God. Yes, Jesus Himself spoke scripture. So, if Jesus fought His battles with the Word, then we should fight our battles speaking the Word also. Find the scriptures that apply

CHAPTER 5: NOT RECEIVING HEALING

to your need, and pray them. Speak what is written. Tell Satan what the Word says.

Satan cannot read your mind. He is not God. He goes by what you say and your reaction to things. You want the air around you to be filled and charged up with the Word of God. Soon, so much Word will be in you, flowing out of you and around you that Satan won't be able to tell the difference between you and Jesus. The Bible also says to remind God of His Word. The Bible says to *put God in remembrance of His Word* (Isaiah 43:26). This is not because God has forgotten what His Word said. It is for us to build up of our faith and to show God that we trust Him and His Word.

Also, angelic hosts are waiting to act on God's Words when we speak them. Speaking the Word is giving commands for the angels of the Lord to move into action in our behalf. They are just waiting for you to speak His Word so that they can go forth and fulfill it. "*Bless the Lord, ye His angels, that excel in strength, do His commandments, hearkening unto the voice of His Word*" (Psalms 103:20). They do not act on our words of unbelief and negative talk but on the Word of God. So it is not just enough to get the Word in; you must speak it out. When you are speaking out loud, you activate the angelic host. You also are hearing yourself, so you are feeding your heart and mind, and strengthening your faith.

YOU ARE HEALED OF THE LORD

The thought may cross your mind that a certain problem runs in your family. Remember, you are now a part of God's family. *Old things are passed away. All things become new* (II Corinthians 5:17). God's family does not have spiritual, physical, mental, or situations that run in the family line. When you make Jesus Lord of your life, you have a new family, a new Father. *You are adopted. You are redeemed from the curse by the blood of Jesus* (Galatians 3:13 and Revelation 5:9). Remember, there is power in the blood of Jesus.

When we study or feed on the Word of God, we are feeding on the bread of life, the very life giving power of Jesus. John 6:33 says, "*Bread of God is He which cometh down from heaven.*" John 1:1 says, "*In the beginning was the Word and the Word was with God and the Word was God.*" Verse 14 goes on to say, "*And the Word was made flesh and dwelt among us.*" In John 6:35, Jesus said, "*I am the bread of life. He that cometh to me shall never hunger.*" We must feed on our bread of life, the Word of God - Jesus. We eat the Word by reading it, studying it, memorizing it, singing it, saying it, and meditating (thinking) on it day and night.

Just like when you break open the wheat berry to get to the nutrition that cleanses and brings health and healing to our bodies, Jesus, our Bread of Life, was broken so we have access to the part of Him that brings forth health

CHAPTER 5: NOT RECEIVING HEALING

and healing and cleanses us spirit, soul, and body. Just like fresh milled grain bread cleanses us, keeps us healthy, and brings life to us, Jesus brings life to us. Remember at the Last Supper, Jesus took the bread and broke it and gave it to His disciples saying, "*This is my body broken for you*" (I Corinthians 11:24). Then His body was broken on the cross for us, and His blood spilled out to cleanse us from all unrighteousness. So, as we partake of the "*Bread of Life,*" Jesus, the Word of God, we are cleansed and healed spirit, soul, and body.

Can your natural body live without eating? It may for a short time. But your body will become weak without food and start dying. It is the same for your spirit. If we don't feed on the Word of God, we start getting spiritually weak and eventually become spiritually dead. Deuteronomy 8:3 says and it is stated again in Matthew 4:4, "… *that He might make thee know that man doth not live by bread only, but by every word that proceedeth out of the mouth of the Lord doth man live.*"

In the tabernacle in the Old Testament, there was the Table of Shewbread. The Shewbread is a symbol of Jesus, the bread of life, who is the Word of God that was made flesh to dwell among us. The Shewbread was to be kept continually on the Table of Shewbread. Shewbread means the "*bread of the face.*" The "face" means the presence. So, we are to get in His presence, feeding on the Word. At this time, only the priest was the only one allowed to eat the Shewbread. Now under the New Testament, we are all priests of the Lord. I Peter 2:9 says, *"But ye are a chosen generation, a royal priesthood, a holy nation, a peculiar people; that ye should show forth the praises of him who hath called you out of darkness into his marvelous light;"* We, His priests, are to eat the Shewbread.

One of the ingredients in the *"bread of life"* is healing and deliverance. Matthew 15:22-28 talks of the Canaanite woman who asks Jesus for healing and deliverance for her daughter. Jesus said, *"It is not meet to take the children's bread, and to cast it to dogs."* Who are the children? God's children are those who have made Jesus Lord of their lives. So, healing and deliverance are in the bread, the Word of God. Psalms 23:5 says, *"Thou preparest a table before me in the presence of mine enemies."* In the presence of our enemies, God is feeding us and giving us life.

Lifestyle and/or Habits

A lot of physical problems can come from our eating, exercise, and hygiene habits, as well as from the things in our environment.

In Leviticus 11, God tells us what we should eat. We should eat things that God created for food. God created a lot of wonderful things for us to eat. Yet, many eat a lot of things God never wanted us to eat, and the things

CHAPTER 5: NOT RECEIVING HEALING

He wants us to eat, they may be prepared (processed) in a way that destroys nutrients. Our society has made it very easy and affordable to eat highly processed foods that are void of nutrition as a result of processing, are full of chemicals and preservatives, and/or mechanically or chemically altered from their original state. They may also contain large amounts of sugar, artificial sweeteners, or chemically produced ingredients. Unless you carefully read the labels of the foods you buy, you may be very surprised at how much of these ingredients you may be consuming.

Lack of exercise can also contribute to health issues. Many are so busy they cannot find time or they just don't exercise. Lives can be full of stress. Exercise helps to reduce stress and keeps our body and heart strong.

So, we should eat what God intended for us to eat and in the form closest to the way He created them and then get regular exercise. Please take time to educate yourself on nutrition and living a healthy lifestyle.

We can also be sick by our hygiene practices, such as hand washing and chemical and food handling. We need to be cognizant of our practices. Also, don't be afraid to speak up if you see a misuse of items or people using bad hygiene practices that can affect you or others. One time when I was at a restaurant, a bowl of cut lemons was sitting on the counter. I saw one of the waitresses pick up a bottle of cleaner and sprayed her rag right over that bowl. So, I immediately got the attention of an employee and explained what happened. I did not point out the employee specifically. I try to be kind about it for I know most people just do things from lack of knowledge or without thinking about what they are doing. We need to be watchful to protect our health and lives.

As we discussed before, lifestyles or habits can open the door to the enemy such as TV and movies we watch, books we read, items we bring into our home, and/or people whom we befriend, and so on. We must also be very careful of books, movies, and so on that even Christians may say are allegories or comparisons to things in the Bible. Some of these are not of God, but demonically inspired. Ask yourself, "Is this God or Satan inspired?" Also ask yourself, "Do these things bring peace, hope, joy, and increase our faith?" Remember, everything has a spiritual source. Whatever activity we are involved in or allow into our home and life, we allow the spiritual influence that those things belong to in our homes and lives as well. Also pray and ask the Lord to protect you and your home and family if you lack knowledge and to help you find the truth in His Word. The truth will set you free. Then listen to your spirit and do what agrees with the Word of God. Be careful to whom you listen. Always listen to the Spirit of God on the inside of you.

CHAPTER 5: NOT RECEIVING HEALING

Strongholds

Some issues we confront, like addictions, bad habits, wrong attitudes, wrong thinking, etc. are strongholds in lives. They began with a wrong choice. They become strongholds when we keep making the same wrong choices. Before long, they have a hold on us. Other strongholds can be generational curses. These healings may only come through fasting (Matthew 17:21).

Besides for myself, the Lord has had me fast for others who had a strongholds or addiction in their lives. They were not in a place to fast for themselves. I had to look at them with these issues like someone who was extremely sick, or even in a coma, as someone who had no strength or could not pray for themselves. If you have ever dealt with someone with an addiction, you know it is an emotional roller coaster. It can be hard to stand for their deliverance. There are extreme emotional highs and lows. One minute, they can think clear, and the next minute, their thinking is irrational. Most of the time, they will not realize how they are behaving. They are not acting of themselves. They are being controlled by the substance or addiction.

While I was fasting for their deliverance, I had a list of scriptures I use in my prayers for them every day. I made the scriptures personal. I would speak the scripture with their name in it. For example, I would speak Psalms

YOU ARE HEALED OF THE LORD

1:1-6 and replace the words "the man" and pronouns "he" and "his" with this person's name or your own. (See Chapter 10, "Pray for Loved Ones", for additional scriptures)

> *"Blessed is _____ who does not walk in the counsel of the ungodly, nor standeth in the way of sinners, nor sitteth in the seat of the scornful. But _____ delight is in the law of the Lord; and in his law doth _____ meditate day and night. And _____ shall be like a tree planted by the rivers of water, that bringeth forth _____ fruit in his season; _____ leaf also shall not wither; and whatever _____ doeth shall prosper. The ungodly are not so: but are like chaff which the wind driveth away. Therefore the wicked shall not stand in the judgment, nor sinners in the congregation of the righteous. For the Lord knoweth the way of the righteous: but the ungodly shall perish."*

I definitely had times I felt like giving up during the process. Occasionally, I didn't think I could not handle the battle any longer. I was ready to give up. The Lord was faithful. He will never leave you comfortless. Often when I was having the hardest time, the Lord would speak an encouraging word to my heart, or He would

CHAPTER 5: NOT RECEIVING HEALING

give me a glimpse of a change in that person, or speak to me through someone else. I would be encouraged to keep pressing on. At other times, though, I had no encouragement to help keep me strong. I had to make a decision, a choice, to keep believing for the healing and deliverance. I would have to stop myself, stop my emotions from overtaking me, and say, "*NO! The Lord told me to do this, so I know He is going to bring the victory. He would not tell me to do something and not keep His word. He puts His word above His name. So, He* will *do this. Satan, you let them go!*" I had to trust the Lord even when I saw no change. I had to trust that if He asked me to do this, He was going to deliver. The more time I spent in God's Word, the stronger I became spiritually and the less I was moved emotionally.

This is true even for our own healing and deliverance. We can get tired and weary in the battle, but the Lord is faithful. Do not give up. Keep running to your Heavenly Father. Keep holding on to the Lord's promises until the answer comes. He will strengthen and help you. You will make it. You are an overcomer in Christ. The Lord is your healer and deliverer.

> Jesus said in Isaiah 61:1, "*The Spirit of the Lord God is upon me; because the Lord hath anointed me to preach good tidings unto the meek; he hath sent me to*

YOU ARE HEALED OF THE LORD

bind up the brokenhearted, to proclaim liberty to the captives, and the opening of the prison to them that are bound."

Jesus came to set us free. That freedom starts with a choice as well. It will not be easy. Once Satan has one bound, he will not give them up easily. In the process toward deliverance, even if a wrong choice is made, get up, keep trusting the Lord, and keep pressing on until freedom comes.

Stand on His word. Seek His face. *Fight*!

CHAPTER 6
THE POWER OF FASTING

THE WORD SHOWS US many reasons and benefits to fasting. Let's look at those that God has revealed to us in Isaiah 58:5-14.

> *"Is it such a fast that I have chosen? A day for man to afflict his soul? Is it to bow down his head as a bulrush? And to spread sackcloth and ashes under him? Wilt thou call this a fast, and an acceptable day to the Lord? Is not this the fast that I have chosen? To loose the bands of wickedness, to undo the heavy burdens, and to let the oppressed go free, and that ye break every yoke? Is it not to deal thy bread to the hungry? And that thou bring the poor that are cast out to thy house?*
>
> *When thou seest the naked, that thou cover him; and that thou hide not thyself from thine own flesh? Then shall thy light break forth as the morning, and thine health shall spring forth speedily: and thy righteousness shall go before thee; the glory of the Lord shall be thy reward.*

YOU ARE HEALED OF THE LORD

Then shalt thou call, and the Lord shall answer; thou shalt cry, and he shall say, "Here I am." If thou take away from the midst of thee the yoke, the putting forth of the finger, and speaking vanity. And if thou draw out thy soul to the hungry, and satisfy the afflicted soul; then shall thy light rise in obscurity, and they darkness be as the noonday.

And the Lord shall guide thee continually, and satisfy thy soul in drought, and make fat thy bones: and thou shalt be like a watered garden, and like a spring of water, whose waters fail not. And they that shall be of thee shall build the old waste places: thou shalt raise up the foundations of many generations; and thou shalt be called the repairer of the breach. The restorer of paths to dwell in.

If thou turn away thy foot from the Sabbath, from doing thy pleasure on my holy day; and call the Sabbath a delight, the holy of the Lord, honorable; and shalt honor him, not doing thine own ways, nor finding thine own pleasure, nor speaking thine own words: Then shalt thou delight thyself in the Lord; and I will cause thee to ride upon the high places of the earth, and feed thee with the heritage of Jacob thy father: For the mouth of the Lord hath spoken it."

CHAPTER 6: THE POWER OF FASTING

This scripture shows us the following reasons and benefits of fasting. (See Chapter 10 for additional scriptures for "Reason and Benefits of Fasting.")

- Directed by the Lord
- Freedom, deliverance, and protection
- Healing
- The presence of the glory of God
- Answered prayers
- Guidance and direction
- Building your faith (See Chapter 10 for scriptures on "Having Faith.")
- Cleansing your physical bodies.

Throughout the Old Testament, when God's people needed deliverance and guidance or for the Lord to move on their behalf, they fasted or called a fast for the people. Several examples include the Israelites deliverance from execution in the time of Esther; Daniel's deliverance from the loin's mouth; the people of Ninevah's deliverance from the wrath of God in the book of Jonah; and Ezra's need for the safe journey for the people in the book of Ezra. The New Testament is also filled with examples of God's people fasting, including Jesus. I recommend looking up the various examples of fasting in the Word. Seeing the mighty hand of God moving is greatly encouraging

Matthew 6:16-21 warns us about making a show of our fast to others. That is drawing attention to yourself for accolades.

> *"Moreover, when ye fast, be not, as the hypocrites, of a sad countenance: for they disfigure their faces, that they may appear unto men to fast. Verily I say unto you, they have their reward. But thou, when thou fastest, anoint thine head, and wash thy face; That thou appear not unto men to fast, but unto thy Father which is in secret: and thy Father, which seeth in secret, shall reward thee openly. Lay not up for yourselves treasures upon earth, where moth and rust doth corrupt, and where thieves break through and steal: But lay up for yourselves treasures in heaven, where neither moth nor rust doth corrupt, and where thieves do not break through nor steal: For where your treasure is, there will your heart be also."*

Fasting is a very powerful part of your walk with the Lord. When we fast, we are telling the Lord that He is more important to us than even the very things that sustain our life. There are many kinds of fasts: the Daniel fast (Daniel 1:12), juice fasts, water-only fasts (not

CHAPTER 6: THE POWER OF FASTING

recommended for a lengthy period unless God specifically directs you and done under a doctor's supervision.), meal fasts, and fasting specific things or activities. Examples of fasting specific things or activities are giving up sugar, caffeine, sodas, TV, movies, or other entertainment. You know what is important in your life. The Lord will honor you in your sincere efforts. A lifestyle of prayer and fasting helps move you out of the way so that God can give you revelations without hindrances from your flesh.

The Lord has had me fast for some of my healings. There are some healings that only happen by prayer and fasting (Matthew 17:21). Yet, not every time I needed healing did the Lord have me fast. When you seek the Lord for your healing process, He will let you know if you should fast. I have also fasted without the Lord's particular instruction when I wanted to know His direction. Isaiah 58:9-11 that when we fast and call upon the Lord, He will answer and guide us continually. The Lord is so faithful to His children and His Word. God is the same yesterday, today, and forever.

CHAPTER 7
SCRIPTURES TO STAND ON FOR ANY HEALING NEED

THE FOLLOWING SCRIPTURES are ones you can stand on for any area of healing, whatever that need may be. These are what I have found in my studies. As you read and study, you may find others that stand out to you and touch your heart. Use those also. You may not find scriptures that mention your exact need, but that does not matter. The Word says, "*By His stripes, I am healed.*" "*He sent His Word to heal them.*" These types of scriptures cover it all. Know in your heart that no matter your need, God wants to heal you.

Any Area of Healing

Genesis 43:28
Exodus 12:13, 23
Exodus 13:14
Exodus 14:13-14
Exodus 15:26
Exodus 23:25-26
Numbers 8:19
Numbers 13:30
Deuteronomy 4:4, 40
Deuteronomy 5:6, 16, 29, 33
Deuteronomy 6:2-3, 17-18, 24

YOU ARE HEALED OF THE LORD

Deuteronomy 7:9, 15
Deuteronomy 8:1
Deuteronomy 11:8-9, 18-21
Deuteronomy 12:28
Deuteronomy 17:20
Deuteronomy 20:3-4
Deuteronomy 28:7, 13
Deuteronomy 30:16, 20
Deuteronomy 32:46-47
Joshua 1:9
Joshua 21:44-45
Joshua 24:17
I Samuel 2:10
I Samuel 3:19
II Samuel 4:9
II Samuel 7:28
II Samuel 8:6b
II Samuel 22:2-4, 17-19, 20, 29-33
I Kings 3:14
I Kings 8:56
II Kings 13:23
II Chronicles 16:9a
Nehemiah 9:6
Job 11:16
Job 33:4
Psalms 1:3
Psalms 5:12
Psalms 18:35
Psalms 20:5-6
Psalms 21:4
Psalms 22:24
Psalms 23:1-6
Psalms 30:2-3, 5
Psalms 32:10
Psalms 33:18-19
Psalms 34:7-8, 10, 15, 19, 22
Psalms 36:6, 7, 9
Psalms 37:4-5, 40
Psalms 40:2, 17
Psalms 41:1-2, 12
Psalms 42:11
Psalms 46:1, 9-10
Psalms 47:1
Psalms 55:22
Psalms 56:9, 13
Psalms 57:2
Psalms 61; 6
Psalms 63:8
Psalms 68:19, 20

CHAPTER 7: SCRIPTURES FOR ANY HEALING

Psalms 69:32
Psalms 71:1, 3, 6
Psalms 73:1
Psalms 84:4, 11, 12
Psalms 90:14, 16
Psalms 91:4, 10, 15-16
Psalms 92:13
Psalms 98:1-2
Psalms 103:2-5
Psalms 105:37
Psalms 106:1
Psalms 107:1, 6, 9, 14, 20
Psalms 115:11, 13-14
Psalms 116:8
Psalms 118:17, 29
Psalms 119:17, 50, 65, 88, 90, 92-93, 114, 116
Psalms 121 (whole)
Psalms 124:8
Psalms 125:1, 2
Psalms 127:1-2
Psalms 128:2, 6
Psalms 130:5
Psalms 138:7, 8
Psalms 139:1-10, 13-19
Psalms 145:16, 19-20
Proverbs 3:1-2, 16-18, 21-22
Proverbs 4:10, 13, 20-22, 23-27
Proverbs 7:2
Proverbs 8:35
Proverbs 9:10-11
Proverbs 10:2, 11, 24, 27
Proverbs 12:18, 28
Proverbs 13:3, 14, 17
Proverbs 14:27, 30
Proverbs 15:4
Proverbs 16:15, 24
Proverbs 18:21
Proverbs 19:23
Proverbs 22:4
Proverbs 28:16
Ecclesiastics 8:5, 12
Isaiah 1:19
Isaiah 3:10
Isaiah 10:27
Isaiah 19:22
Isaiah 25:4, 8
Isaiah 30:18
Isaiah 40:26

YOU ARE HEALED OF THE LORD

Isaiah 41:10
Isaiah 43:1
Isaiah 44:2a
Isaiah 46:4
Isaiah 53:4-5
Isaiah 54:17
Isaiah 55:3
Isaiah 57:18, 19
Isaiah 58:8
Isaiah 59:1, 19
Isaiah 60:2
Isaiah 62:4
Jeremiah 7:23
Jeremiah 16:21
Jeremiah 17:7-8, 14
Jeremiah 29:11
Jeremiah 30:17
Jeremiah 31:3-4, 9, 16-17
Jeremiah 32:27, 41
Jeremiah 33:6
Jeremiah 38:20
Jeremiah 50:34
Ezekiel 12:28
Ezekiel 18:5-9, 19, 27, 28
Ezekiel 33:15-16
Ezekiel 36:11
Ezekiel 37:14

Daniel 10:12
Hosea 6:1
Hosea 13:9, 14
Joel 2:25
Joel 3:16
Amos 5:4, 14, 15
Nahum 1:7, 13
Zechariah 1:3
Zechariah 2:8
Malachi 2:5
Malachi 4:2
Matthew 4:16, 23-24
Matthew 6:33
Matthew 7:7-11
Matthew 8:7, 13, 16-17
Matthew 9:35
Matthew 10:1, 8
Matthew 12:15
Matthew 13:15
Matthew 14:14, 36
Matthew 16:18-19
Matthew 18:18, 19-20
Matthew 19:2, 26
Matthew 21:21-22
Mark 1:34
Mark 3:15
Mark 5:34

CHAPTER 7: SCRIPTURES FOR ANY HEALING

Mark 6:13, 56
Mark 9:23
Mark 10:52a
Mark 11:22-26
Mark 14:36A
Mark 16:16-18
Luke 1:37, 45, 68
Luke 4:18, 40
Luke 5:17
Luke 6:19
Luke 7:2-3, 10, 21
Luke 8:46
Luke 9:1-2, 6, 11
Luke 10:19
Luke 11:11-13
Luke 12:6-7, 32
Luke 17:6
Luke 18:1-8, 27
Luke 21:18
John 1:4
John 4:47, 50-51
John 5:5, 8-9, 24
John 6:48, 51
John 10:28
John 11:22, 25
John 14:12-14
John 15:3, 7
John 16:23-24
John 17:23
John 20:31
Acts 3:16
Acts 4:14, 22
Acts 5:15-16
Acts 10:38
Acts 16:31
Acts 17:25, 28
Acts 19:12
Acts 28:9, 27
Romans 4:17, 21
Romans 5:5, 17
Romans 6:8-9
Romans 8:2, 6, 10-11, 13, 26, 28, 31-32, 37
Romans 9:17, 33
Romans 10:11-13
Romans 12:2, 12
Romans 15:4
Romans 16:20
I Corinthians 1:9
I Corinthians 2:9
I Corinthians 6:14, 19
I Corinthians 12:8-11
I Corinthians 15:22, 54-55, 57

YOU ARE HEALED OF THE LORD

II Corinthians 1:9-10
II Corinthians 2:14
II Corinthians 3:6
II Corinthians 10:4-5
II Corinthians 12:9
Galatians 3:13-14
Galatians 3:22, 28-29
Galatians 4:7
Galatians 5:1
Ephesians 1:3, 19-21
Ephesians 3:20
Ephesians 4:7
Philippians 1:6
Philippians 2:9-11, 14-16
Philippians 3:21
Philippians 4:6, 7-8, 13, 19
Colossians 1:13
Colossians 2:10
II Thessalonians 3:3
II Timothy 1:12
II Timothy 4:18
Philemon 6
Hebrews 2:8a
Hebrews 4:15-16
Hebrews 5:7
Hebrews 6:18
Hebrews 7:25
Hebrews 10:19-23, 35-36
Hebrews 11:1, 6
Hebrews 12:2
Hebrews 13:8, 21
James 4:7
James 5:14-15, 16
I Peter 1:18-21
I Peter 2:6, 9, 24
I Peter 5:7
II Peter 1:3-4
I John 2:14
I John 3:22
I John 4:4
I John 5:12, 14-15
II John 2
Revelation 1:17-18
Revelation 2:7
Revelation 3:20
Revelation 5:9
Revelation 7:17
Revelation 12:11
Revelation 22:17

CHAPTER 8

SCRIPTURES TO STAND ON FOR SPECIFIC AREAS OF HEALING OF YOUR PHYSICAL BODY

THE FOLLOWING ARE scriptures that I have found for you to stand on for specific areas of healing in your physical body. Even if you do not find your specific need listed, all you need to know and believe is that the work that Jesus did on the cross covers every need you could ever have. By His stripes, we were healed.

Anorexia

Psalms 92:14   Isaiah 58:11

Arthritis

Psalms 18:1   Proverbs 3:7-8
Psalms 20:8   Proverbs 16:24
Psalms 71:16   Isaiah 35:3
Psalms 105:37   Isaiah 58:11
Psalms 144:1   Isaiah 66:14
Psalms 146:8   Ezekiel 37:4-5

YOU ARE HEALED OF THE LORD

Zechariah 8:9, 13
Matthew 11:5
Matthew 12:10, 13
Matthew 15:30
Mark 3:1, 5

Luke 6:6, 10
Luke 13:11-13
Acts 3:6-8
Acts 8:7
Hebrews 12:12

Back Problems

Psalms 18:1
Psalms 20:8
Psalms 71:16
Psalms 105:37
Psalms 146:8

Proverbs 3:7-8
Proverbs 16:24
Isaiah 58:11
Ezekiel 37:5
Luke 13:11-13

Bites

Acts 28:3-6

Blindness – See Eye Problems

Blood Disorders/Problems

Leviticus 17:14
Psalms 72:14
Proverbs 3:7-8
Joel 3:21

Matthew 9:20-22
Mark 5:25-29
Acts 28:8

CHAPTER 8: SCRIPTURES FOR BODY

Bones

Psalms 34:20
Psalms 105:37
Psalms 146:8
Proverbs 3:7-8
Proverbs 16:24
Isaiah 58:11
Isaiah 66:14
Ezekiel 37:5
Matthew 15:30
Luke 13:11-13
Acts 3:6-8

Bowel Problems (Also see Stomach Problems)

Proverbs 3:7-8
Acts 28:8

Breathing Problems

Genesis 2:7
Job 12:10
Job 27:3
Job 33:4
Psalms 33:6
Isaiah 42:5
Ezekiel 37:5
Daniel 5:23b
Acts 17:25

Child Baring/Barrenness

Genesis 9:1, 7
Genesis 17:6-7
Genesis 21:2
Genesis 25:21
Genesis 26:24
Genesis 28:3-4, 14
Genesis 30:23
Genesis 35:11
Genesis 48:4
Genesis 49:25

YOU ARE HEALED OF THE LORD

Exodus 1:7, 20
Exodus 23:26
Leviticus 26:9
Deuteronomy 1:11
Deuteronomy 6:2-3
Deuteronomy 7:12-14
Deuteronomy 8:1
Deuteronomy 12:23-25, 28
Deuteronomy 13:17
Deuteronomy 28:4, 11
Deuteronomy 30:16
Judges 13:3, 5
I Samuel 1:20
I Samuel 2:21
II Samuel 7:12
Psalms 71:6
Psalms 92:14
Psalms 105:24
Psalms 127:3-5
Psalms 128:3
Psalms 139:13-18
Psalms 147:13
Isaiah 54:2-3
Jeremiah 30:19-20
Ezekiel 36:11
Matthew 1:18
Matthew 9:20-22
Mark 5:25-29
Luke 1:7, 13, 24a, 30-31
Hebrews 11:11

Chronic Ailments
Mark 5:25-29
Mark 9:21, 23, 25
John 5:5, 8-9
John 9:1, 6-7
Acts 3:2, 6-8

Coma
Mark 5:39-42

CHAPTER 8: SCRIPTURES FOR BODY

Crippled

Psalms 18:33
Psalms 20:8
Psalms 71:16
Psalms 105:37
Psalms 146:8
Proverbs 3:7-8
Habakkuk 3:19
Matthew 4:24
Matthew 8:6, 8, 13
Matthew 9:2, 6-7
Matthew 11:5
Matthew 12:10, 13
Matthew 15:30
Matthew 21:14
Mark 3:1, 5
Luke 6:6, 10
Luke 13:11-13
Acts 3:2, 6-8
Acts 8:7
Acts 9:33-34
Acts 14:8-10
Hebrews 12:12-13

Dead Raised (if God can do this, He can heal)

II Kings 4:32-33, 35
Matthew 9:18, 25
Matthew 11:5
Mark 5:35-42
Luke 7:12-15
Luke 8:54-55
Acts 9:37, 40
Acts 20:9-10
Romans 4:17
I Corinthians 6:14
II Corinthians 1:9-10

Deformities

Psalms 146:8
Matthew 11:5
Matthew 12:10, 13
Matthew 15:30
Matthew 21:14
Mark 3:1, 5

YOU ARE HEALED OF THE LORD

Luke 6:6, 10
Luke 13:11-13
Luke 22:50-51
Acts 3:2, 6-8

Acts 8:7
Acts 14:8-10
Hebrews 12:12-13

Drinking/Ingesting Poisons
Mark 16:18

Dysentery – See Bowel Problems

Ear Problems
Psalms 92:11
Proverbs 20:12
Isaiah 29:18
Isaiah 32:3
Isaiah 35:5
Isaiah 42:18
Jeremiah 13:15
Jeremiah 28:7
Ezekiel 24:26

Ezekiel 44:5
Matthew 11:5
Matthew 13:9, 16, 43
Mark 4:9
Mark 7:32-35, 37
Mark 9:25
Luke 22:50-51
Revelation 2:7

Eating Disorders
Deuteronomy 6:11
Deuteronomy 12:7
Nehemiah 8:10

Psalms 78:29
Psalms 103:5
Psalms 128:2

CHAPTER 8: SCRIPTURES FOR BODY

Epilepsy

Matthew 4:24 Matthew 17:15, 18-21

Eye Problems

Deuteronomy 34:7
Psalms 36:9
Psalms 92:11
Psalms 146:8
Proverbs 20:12
Isaiah 29:18
Isaiah 32:3
Isaiah 33:17
Isaiah 35:5
Isaiah 42:7, 16, 18
Ezekiel 44:5
Malachi 1:5
Matthew 9:27-30
Matthew 11:5
Matthew 12:22
Matthew 13:16
Matthew 15:30
Matthew 20:30-34
Matthew 21:14
Mark 8:22-25
Mark 10:46, 51-52
Luke 4:18
Luke 7:21
Luke 18:35, 38, 41-43
John 9:1, 6-7

Feet Problems - See Walking Problems

Female Organ Problems

Matthew 9:20-22 Luke 8:43-44, 47-48
Mark 5:25-29

YOU ARE HEALED OF THE LORD

Fever
Matthew 8:15
Mark 1:30-31
Luke 4:38-39
Acts 28:8

Hands
Genesis 49:24
Psalms 144:1
Isaiah 35:3
Zechariah 8:9, 13
Matthew 12:10, 13
Mark 3:1, 5
Hebrews 12:12

Hearing Problems – See Ear Problems

Heart Problems
Psalms 27:13-14
Psalms 31:24
Psalms 69:32
Psalms 73:26
Psalms 108:1
Psalms 119:32
Isaiah 57:15

Hemorrhaging
Matthew 9:20-22
Mark 5:25-29
Luke 8:43-44, 47-48

Hemorrhoids - See Bowel Problems

Intestinal Problems - See Bowel Problems

Joint Problems - See Arthritis or Walking Problems

Leg Problems - See Walking Problems

CHAPTER 8: SCRIPTURES FOR BODY

Malaria

Matthew 8:15
Mark 1:30-31
Luke 4:38-39
Acts 28:8

Memory Problems

Matthew 4:24
I Corinthians 2:16
Philippians 2:5
II Timothy 1:7

Mental Problems

Psalms 71:1
Isaiah 32:4
Daniel 4:33-34
Matthew 4:24
Matthew 17:15, 18
I Corinthians 2:16
II Corinthians 10:4-5
Philippians 2:5
Philippians 4:7-8
II Timothy 1:7

Muscle Problems – See Strength Problems

Paralysis

Matthew 4:24
Matthew 8:6-8, 13
Matthew 9:2, 6-7
Matthew 15:30
Mark 2:3, 11-12
Luke 5:18, 24-25
Acts 8:7
Acts 9:33-34
Acts 14:8-10

Skin Problems

Exodus 4:7	Matthew 8:2-3
Exodus 15:26	Matthew 11:5
II Kings 5:1, 10, 14	Mark 1:40-42
Job 2:7	Luke 5:12-13
Job 42:10	Luke 17:12-16, 19

Sleep Problems

Exodus 23:12	Psalms 127:2
Exodus 31:15	Proverbs 3:24
Exodus 33:14	Proverbs 6:20-22
Exodus 34:21	Isaiah 30:15
Leviticus 23:3	Isaiah 32:18
Leviticus 26:6	Jeremiah 31:2, 26
I Kings 8:56	Jeremiah 50:34
Joshua 21:44-45	Ezekiel 34:25
Psalms 3:5	Hosea 2:18
Psalms 4:8	Matthew 11:28-30
Psalms 16:9	Mark 4:38-39
Psalms 23:2	Mark 6:31
Psalms 37:7-9	Acts 12:6
Psalms 116:7	Hebrews 4:3, 9

CHAPTER 8: SCRIPTURES FOR BODY

Speech Problems

Exodus 4:12, 15
Psalms 19:14
Isaiah 32:4
Isaiah 35:6
Isaiah 41:1
Ezekiel 24:27

Matthew 9:33
Matthew 12:22
Matthew 15:30
Mark 7:32-35, 37
Mark 9:25

Stomach Problems (Also see Bowel Problems)

Deuteronomy 6:11
Deuteronomy 12:7
Nehemiah 8:10
Psalms 78:29
Psalms 92:14
Psalms 103:5

Psalms 128:2
Proverbs 3:7-8
Isaiah 58:11
Mark 16:18

Strength Problems

Genesis 49:24
Exodus 1:20
Exodus 15:2
Deuteronomy 11:8
Deuteronomy 33:25
Deuteronomy 34:7
Judges 15:14

Judges 16:3
I Samuel 2:4, 10b
II Samuel 22:33
I Chronicles 22:13
I Chronicles 28:20
I Chronicles 29:11-12
Nehemiah 8:10

YOU ARE HEALED OF THE LORD

Job 12:13, 16
Job 17:9
Job 36:5
Psalms 18:1-2, 32, 39
Psalms 19:14
Psalms 20:8
Psalms 22:19
Psalms 27:1, 13-14
Psalms 28:7-8
Psalms 29:11
Psalms 37:39
Psalms 46:1
Psalms 59:16-17
Psalms 62:7
Psalms 68:28, 35
Psalms 71:16
Psalms 80:17, 18
Psalms 81:1
Psalms 84:5
Psalms 86:16
Psalms 89:20-23
Psalms 105:24, 37
Psalms 118:14
Psalms 119:28
Psalms 125:1
Psalms 138:3
Psalms 140:7
Psalms 144:1
Psalms 146:8
Proverbs 8:14
Proverbs 10:29
Proverbs 20:29
Isaiah 12:2
Isaiah 26:4
Isaiah 27:5
Isaiah 30:15
Isaiah 35:3
Isaiah 40:29, 31
Isaiah 41:1, 10
Jeremiah 16:19
Daniel 10:18-19
Joel 3:16
Micah 5:4
Habakkuk 3:19
Haggai 2:4
Zechariah 4:6
Zechariah 8:13
Zechariah 10:6
Matthew 11:5
Matthew 15:30
Luke 13:11-13
Acts 3:7

CHAPTER 8: SCRIPTURES FOR BODY

Philippians 4:13
Colossians 1:11
Hebrews 12:12

Swelling Problems
Nehemiah 9:21
Luke 14:2-4

Walking Problems
Psalms 18:33, 36
Psalms 20:8
Psalms 71:16
Psalms 94:18
Psalms 105:37
Psalms 146:8
Proverbs 3:23
Isaiah 35:3, 6, 9
Isaiah 40:31
Ezekiel 37:5
Habakkuk 3:19
Zechariah 3:7
Matthew 4:24
Matthew 8:6, 8, 13
Matthew 9:2, 6-7
Matthew 11:5
Matthew 15:30
Matthew 21:14
Luke 5:18, 24-25
Luke 7:22
Luke 13:11-13
John 5:5, 8-9
Acts 3:2, 6-8
Acts 8:7
Acts 9:33-34
Acts 14:8-10
Hebrews 12:12

Water Retention
Luke 14:2-4

CHAPTER 9
SCRIPTURES TO STAND ON FOR SPECIFIC AREAS OF HEALING FOR YOUR MIND, WILL, AND EMOTIONS

Condemnation

Leviticus 11:45
Leviticus 21:8
Leviticus 22:32
II Chronicles 30:9, 18-20
Psalms 19:14
Psalms 51:17
Psalms 86:17
Psalms 94:14
Psalms 103:3, 8, 12
Psalms 119:9, 11, 28, 45, 133
Psalms 125:1
Psalms 130:4, 8
Psalms 139:1-18
Isaiah 45:25
Isaiah 54:4
Isaiah 61:10
Isaiah 62:2-4
Isaiah 66:5
Jeremiah 3:22
Jeremiah 31:33-34
Jeremiah 33:8
Ezekiel 18:22
Ezekiel 33:11, 15-16
Ezekiel 36:23-36
Ezekiel 37:23
Hosea 14:4
Joel 2:13
Micah 7:18-19
Zephaniah 3:16-17, 20
Zechariah 3:4

YOU ARE HEALED OF THE LORD

Matthew 9:6-7
Matthew 11:28-30
Luke 4:18
John 5:24
John 11:25
John 12:46
John 16:33
John 20:31
Acts 10:43
Acts 13:39
Acts 16:31
Romans 3:3-4
Romans 5:1, 17, 20
Romans 6:8-13
Romans 8:2, 6
Romans 9:33
Romans 10:9

Galatians 3:13-14
Galatians 4:5-6
Ephesians 2:1-10
Philippians 2:5
Philippians 3:9
Colossians 1:13-14, 20-21
Colossians 2:10
I Thessalonians 5:23
II Timothy 3:15
James 3:18
I Peter 1:18-19
I Peter 2:24
I John 1:9
I John 4:10
I John 5:1
Jude 24

Demon Possession (Free from)

Matthew 4:24
Matthew 8:16, 28, 32
Matthew 9:33
Matthew 12:22
Matthew 15:22-28
Matthew 17:18-21
Matthew 18:18

Mark 1:23, 25-26, 34, 39
Mark 3:15
Mark 5:2, 8, 13
Mark 6:13
Mark 7:29
Mark 9:25
Mark 16:17

CHAPTER 9: SCRIPTURES FOR MIND

Luke 4:33, 35
Luke 6:18
Luke 7:21
Luke 8:2, 27, 33, 35-36
Luke 9:38, 42
Luke 11:14

Acts 5:15-16
Acts 8:7
Acts 16:16, 18
Acts 19:12
Colossians 1:13-14
James 4:7

Depression/Hopelessness

Exodus 15:2
Numbers 13:20
Deuteronomy 31:23
Joshua 1:6a
II Samuel 10:12
I Chronicles 19:13
I Chronicles 22:13
I Chronicles 28:20
Nehemiah 12:43
Job 11:16
Psalms 3:3-4
Psalms 4:6-7
Psalms 9:10
Psalms 27:13-14
Psalms 28:7
Psalms 31:24
Psalms 34:18
Psalms 39:7

Psalms 42:5
Psalms 62:10-11
Psalms 71:1, 21
Psalms 72:7
Psalms 121 (whole)
Psalms 138:3
Psalms 147:3
Isaiah 14:3, 25b
Isaiah 25:8
Isaiah 26:3
Isaiah 40:31
Isaiah 51:3, 11
Isaiah 53:4-5
Isaiah 57:15, 18
Isaiah 58:11
Isaiah 60:20
Isaiah 61:1
Isaiah 65:19

YOU ARE HEALED OF THE LORD

Luke 4:18
Luke 7:13
Acts 20:32
Romans 8:6
Romans 15:13
II Corinthians 1:3

II Corinthians 10:4-5
Philippians 2:5
Philippians 4:7-8
Colossians 3:15
Jude 24

Fear

Genesis 15:1
Genesis 21:17
Genesis 26:24
Genesis 43:23a
Genesis 46:3
Exodus 14:13-14
Exodus 23:27
Exodus 33:22
Leviticus 26:5-6
Numbers 6:24-26
Numbers 14:9
Deuteronomy 1:21, 29-30
Deuteronomy 3:22
Deuteronomy 9:3
Deuteronomy 11:25
Deuteronomy 20:3-4
Deuteronomy 31:6, 8
Joshua 1:9

Joshua 8:1
Joshua 23:10
Judges 6:23
II Samuel 22:2-4, 5-19
I Kings 17:13a
II Kings 6:16
II Kings 17:37-39
I Chronicles 22:13
I Chronicles 28:20
II Chronicles 32:7-8
Ezra 10:4
Job 5:19, 21
Job 11:14-15
Job 21:9
Job 37:23
Job 39:22
Psalms 3:3-4, 6
Psalms 4:8

CHAPTER 9: SCRIPTURES FOR MIND

Psalms 5:12
Psalms 8:6
Psalms 9:9-10
Psalms 16:8
Psalms 17:8
Psalms 18:2-3
Psalms 23:4
Psalms 27:1, 13-14
Psalms 31:5, 11-14, 20
Psalms 33:20
Psalms 34:4, 7-8, 17
Psalms 37:6-10, 39
Psalms 44:4
Psalms 46:1-11
Psalms 49:5
Psalms 55:22
Psalms 56:3-4, 11
Psalms 62:1-2
Psalms 71:3
Psalms 84:11
Psalms 91:5, 8-10, 11
Psalms 94:19
Psalms 107:13, 29
Psalms 112:6, 7-8
Psalms 116:7
Psalms 118:5-6
Psalms 119:114, 117
Psalms 121 (whole)
Psalms 138:3, 7
Psalms 139:5, 7-10
Psalms 144:2
Proverbs 1:33
Proverbs 3:24-26
Proverbs 12:21, 28
Proverbs 24:19-20
Proverbs 29:25
Ecclesiastes 8:5
Isaiah 7:4a
Isaiah 8:12b
Isaiah 12:2
Isaiah 14:3
Isaiah 26:3
Isaiah 32:18
Isaiah 33:16
Isaiah 35:3-7
Isaiah 41:10, 13, 14
Isaiah 43:1-3
Isaiah 44:2, 8
Isaiah 46:4
Isaiah 51:7, 12, 15-16
Isaiah 54:4, 14-17
Isaiah 57:11
Jeremiah 17:7
Jeremiah 23:4

YOU ARE HEALED OF THE LORD

Jeremiah 29:11
Jeremiah 30:10-11a
Jeremiah 46:27-28a
Lamentations 3:57
Daniel 6:22-23
Daniel 10:19
Joel 2:21
Nahum 1:7
Zephaniah 3:16-17
Haggai 1:13
Haggai 2:5
Zechariah 2:5, 8
Zechariah 8:13, 15
Zechariah 9:12
Matthew 8:26-27
Matthew 10:28-31
Matthew 11:28-30
Matthew 14:27
Matthew 28:5
Mark 6:50
Luke 1:74, 78-79
Luke 2:10, 13-14
Luke 8:50
Luke 10:19
Luke 12:4, 6-7, 32
Luke 21:18
John 14:1, 27
John 16:33
Romans 8:15, 28, 35, 37-39
Romans 12:21
Romans 16:20
I Corinthians 2:16
I Corinthians 16:10
II Corinthians 2:14
II Corinthians 7:6
II Corinthians 10:4-5
Galatians 1:3-4
Philippians 1:14, 28
Philippians 2:5
Philippians 4:6, 7-8
II Thessalonians 2:16-17
II Thessalonians 3:3, 16
II Timothy 1:7
II Timothy 4:18
Hebrews 4:3
Hebrews 13:6
James 4:7
I Peter 5:7
I John 4:18
Revelation 12:11

CHAPTER 9: SCRIPTURES FOR MIND

Joy

Exodus 15:2
Deuteronomy 12:7
Deuteronomy 16:11
Joshua 6:20
Nehemiah 8:10
Job 33:26
Psalms 4:7
Psalms 5:11
Psalms 16:8-9, 11
Psalms 20:5
Psalms 21:1, 6
Psalms 30:5, 11
Psalms 32:11
Psalms 34:1
Psalms 35:9, 27-28
Psalms 45:7, 15
Psalms 47:1
Psalms 59:16-17
Psalms 68:3
Psalms 69:30
Psalms 70:4
Psalms 92:4
Psalms 94:19
Psalms 100:1-5
Psalms 104:34
Psalms 105:43
Psalms 118:15-16, 24
Psalms 126:2, 5
Psalms 128:2
Psalms 132:16
Psalms 136:3-4
Psalms 138:5
Psalms 144:15
Psalms 146:5
Proverbs 3:13, 18
Proverbs 12:20, 25
Proverbs 14:21
Proverbs 15:13, 15, 23
Proverbs 16:20
Proverbs 17:22
Proverbs 18:21
Proverbs 28:14
Proverbs 29:18
Ecclesiastes 2:26
Ecclesiastes 3:13, 22
Ecclesiastes 5:18
Ecclesiastes 9:9
Isaiah 12:2-3
Isaiah 25:8
Isaiah 35:10

YOU ARE HEALED OF THE LORD

Isaiah 51:3, 11
Isaiah 52:9
Isaiah 53:4-5
Isaiah 55:12
Isaiah 60:18
Isaiah 61:1, 3, 10
Isaiah 65:18, 19
Isaiah 66:14
Jeremiah 15:16
Jeremiah 30:19
Jeremiah 31:12-13
Joel 2:21
Zephaniah 3:14
Zechariah 2:10
Zechariah 9:9
Zechariah 10:7
Matthew 2:10
Matthew 14:27
Luke 1:47
Luke 2:10, 13-14
Luke 10:20
John 15:11
John 16:20, 22, 24
John 17:13
Acts 2:46
Acts 8:39
Acts 11:23
Acts 14:17
Acts 16:34
Romans 5:2
Romans 8:28
Romans 12:15
Romans 14:17
Romans 15:13
II Corinthians 2:3
Philippians 4:4
I Thessalonians 5:16
Revelation 7:17

Peace

Genesis 43:23
Exodus 14:14
Leviticus 26:6
Numbers 6:24-26
Numbers 25:12
Deuteronomy 31:6, 8
Joshua 21:44-45
Judges 6:23
I Samuel 25:6
I Kings 2:33b

CHAPTER 9: SCRIPTURES FOR MIND

I Kings 8:56
Job 22:21
Psalms 4:8
Psalms 23:2, 4
Psalms 29:11
Psalms 34:14
Psalms 37:7-9, 11, 37
Psalms 42:5, 11
Psalms 46:10-11
Psalms 55:18
Psalms 62:1-2
Psalms 72:3, 7
Psalms 85:8
Psalms 94:19
Psalms 107:29
Psalms 116:7
Psalms 119:165
Psalms 122:7
Psalms 125:5
Psalms 147:12-18
Proverbs 3:1-2, 16-18
Proverbs 16:7
Isaiah 9:7
Isaiah 14:3
Isaiah 26:3, 12
Isaiah 27:5
Isaiah 32:17-18
Isaiah 39:8
Isaiah 48:18
Isaiah 51:3, 12
Isaiah 53:4-5
Isaiah 54:10, 13
Isaiah 55:12
Isaiah 57:15, 19
Isaiah 58:11
Isaiah 61:1, 3
Isaiah 66:13
Jeremiah 29:11
Jeremiah 31:2
Jeremiah 33:6
Jeremiah 50:34
Ezekiel 34:25
Ezekiel 37:26
Daniel 4:1
Daniel 10:18-19
Haggai 2:9
Zechariah 2:10
Malachi 2:5
Matthew 6:25-27
Matthew 11:28-30
Mark 4:39
Mark 5:34
Luke 1:79
Luke 2:10, 13-14

YOU ARE HEALED OF THE LORD

Luke 4:18
Luke 24:36
John 14:1, 18, 27
John 16:33
Acts 10:36
Romans 2:10
Romans 5:1-2
Romans 8:6, 28
Romans 10:15
Romans 12:18
Romans 14:17
Romans 15:13, 33
Romans 16:20
I Corinthians 1:3
I Corinthians 14:33
II Corinthians 1:2, 3
II Corinthians 7:6
II Corinthians 10:4-5
II Corinthians 13:11, 14
Galatians 1:3-4
Galatians 5:22-23
Ephesians 1:2
Ephesians 2:14
Ephesians 4:3
Philippians 1:2
Philippians 4:6, 7-8
Colossians 1:2, 20
Colossians 3:15-17
I Thessalonians 1:1
I Thessalonians 5:13, 23
II Thessalonians 3:16
I Timothy 2:2-3
II Timothy 2:22
Hebrews 4:3, 9
James 3:17
I Peter 3:11
I Peter 5:7
II Peter 1:2

Protection

Genesis 28:15
Exodus 14:13-14
Exodus 15:3, 6-8
Exodus 23:22, 27
Exodus 33:22
Numbers 10:35
Deuteronomy 1:29-30
Deuteronomy 3:22
Deuteronomy 11:23-25
Deuteronomy 20:1, 4
Deuteronomy 23:9, 14
Deuteronomy 28:7

CHAPTER 9: SCRIPTURES FOR MIND

Deuteronomy 33:27, 29
Joshua 1:9
Joshua 10:25
Joshua 21:44-45
Joshua 23:10
Judges 3:9, 15a
I Samuel 12:11b
I Samuel 20:21
II Samuel 7:3
II Samuel 8:6
II Samuel 22:2-4, 5-20, 30, 49-51
II Kings 6:16, 17
II Kings 17:39
I Chronicles 17:8
I Chronicles 28:20
II Chronicles 16:9a
II Chronicles 20:29
II Chronicles 32:7-8
Ezra 8:31
Nehemiah 4:20
Nehemiah 9:6
Job 3:23
Job 5:19, 21
Job 11:18
Job 19:25
Psalms 3:3-4, 6-8
Psalms 5:12
Psalms 7:10
Psalms 9:3
Psalms 12:5
Psalms 15:1-5
Psalms 17:7-8
Psalms 18:2-3, 16-19, 27, 30, 33, 35, 48
Psalms 20:5-6
Psalms 21:7
Psalms 23:5-6
Psalms 24:8
Psalms 27:3, 5
Psalms 28:7
Psalms 31:5, 20
Psalms 32:7
Psalms 33:18-19, 20
Psalms 34:4, 7-8, 17, 19
Psalms 36:6
Psalms 37:1-2, 7-9, 17, 19-20, 40
Psalms 40:2
Psalms 41:1-2
Psalms 44:5
Psalms 55:16-17, 22
Psalms 56:13
Psalms 59:9, 16-17

YOU ARE HEALED OF THE LORD

Psalms 60:12
Psalms 61:3-4
Psalms 62:1-2, 7
Psalms 63:8
Psalms 66:9
Psalms 68:1-2
Psalms 71:3, 7
Psalms 72:14
Psalms 84:11
Psalms 89:18, 20-23
Psalms 91:1-16
Psalms 94:18
Psalms 98:1-2
Psalms 103:4
Psalms 105:14-15
Psalms 106:8, 10
Psalms 107:2, 6, 13, 29
Psalms 108:13
Psalms 115:9, 11
Psalms 116:8
Psalms 118:5-6, 12-13, 21
Psalms 119:114, 117
Psalms 121:1-8
Psalms 122:2
Psalms 124:7-8
Psalms 125:1-3
Psalms 129:3-4
Psalms 138:7
Psalms 139:7-18
Psalms 142:5
Psalms 144:2
Psalms 145:20
Proverbs 1:33
Proverbs 2:7-8
Proverbs 3:21-26
Proverbs 4:5-7
Proverbs 10:30
Proverbs 11:8
Proverbs 12:21
Proverbs 14:26-27
Proverbs 16:7
Proverbs 18:10
Proverbs 19:23
Proverbs 21:31
Proverbs 22:5
Proverbs 24:19-20
Proverbs 29:25
Proverbs 30:5
Ecclesiastes 8:5
Isaiah 14:30a
Isaiah 25:4, 8
Isaiah 30:15
Isaiah 31:5
Isaiah 32:2, 18

CHAPTER 9: SCRIPTURES FOR MIND

Isaiah 33:16, 22
Isaiah 35:4, 9
Isaiah 37:35
Isaiah 40:26
Isaiah 41:10, 14
Isaiah 42:6
Isaiah 43:1-3, 14, 16, 18-19
Isaiah 46:4
Isaiah 47:4
Isaiah 51:3, 15-16
Isaiah 52:10
Isaiah 54:14, 17
Isaiah 59:19-20
Isaiah 60:2, 18
Isaiah 63:9
Isaiah 65:25
Jeremiah 5:14
Jeremiah 16:19
Jeremiah 23:6
Jeremiah 30:10-11
Jeremiah 31:11
Jeremiah 32:37
Jeremiah 33:16
Jeremiah 50:34
Ezekiel 3:9
Ezekiel 28:26
Ezekiel 34:27-28
Daniel 3:17
Daniel 6:22-23
Nahum 1:7, 13
Haggai 1:13
Zechariah 2:5, 8
Zechariah 8:7
Zechariah 9:12, 15
Zechariah 10:6
Zechariah 12:8
Zechariah 14:3
Matthew 26:53
Mark 4:39
Luke 1:69, 71-72, 74
Luke 10:19
Luke 21:18
John 17:12
Acts 27:24
Romans 8:35, 37
Romans 16:25
II Corinthians 10:4-5
Galatians 1:3-4
Colossians 1:13
II Thessalonians 3:3
II Timothy 4:18
Hebrews 7:25
Hebrews 13:6
I Peter 3:13

CHAPTER 10
SCRIPTURES LISTS REFERRED TO THROUGHOUT THIS BOOK

Answering Prayers

Deuteronomy 4:29-31
Psalms 3:3-4
Psalms 4:3
Psalms 6:9
Psalms 10:17
Psalms 17:6
Psalms 18:6-17
Psalms 20:5-6
Psalms 21:2
Psalms 22:24
Psalms 34:4, 15, 17
Psalms 37:4-5
Psalms 55:16-17
Psalms 57:2-3
Psalms 65:5
Psalms 86:7
Psalms 91:15
Psalms 116:1-2
Psalms 118:5-6, 21
Psalms 120:1
Psalms 121:1-2
Psalms 138:3
Psalms 145:18, 19
Proverbs 8:17
Proverbs 15:8, 29
Ecclesiastes 5:20
Isaiah 41:17
Isaiah 58:9
Isaiah 65:24
Jeremiah 29:12-14
Jeremiah 33:3
Daniel 10:12

YOU ARE HEALED OF THE LORD

Zechariah 10:6
Matthew 6:8
Matthew 7:7-8
Matthew 18:18
Matthew 21:21-22
Luke 11:13
John 15:7
Ephesians 3:20
Hebrews 5:7
James 4:2-3
I Peter 3:12

Deliverance by God

Genesis 45:7
Exodus 13:9, 14, 21-22
Exodus 14:13-14
Exodus 15:6-8, 16
Leviticus 26:6, 13
Numbers 10:35
Numbers 15:41
Deuteronomy 1:29-30
Deuteronomy 4:29-30
Deuteronomy 5:6
Deuteronomy 7:8-9, 12-13
Deuteronomy 9:3
Deuteronomy 10:21
Deuteronomy 20:3-4
Deuteronomy 28:7
Deuteronomy 31:6
Joshua 21:44-45
Joshua 23:10
Judges 3:9a, 15a
I Samuel 2:8-9
I Samuel 12:11
I Samuel 14:6
II Samuel 4:9
II Samuel 22:2-4, 17-19, 20, 29-33, 49
I Kings 6:12-13
I Chronicles 29:11-12
II Chronicles 32:7-8
Ezra 8:31
Nehemiah 9:6
Psalms 7:10
Psalms 8:6
Psalms 16:8
Psalms 18:6-17, 19, 27, 35, 50

CHAPTER 10: SCRIPTURES LISTS

Psalms 20:8
Psalms 23:1-6
Psalms 33:18-19, 20
Psalms 34:4, 17, 19
Psalms 37:20a, 28, 40
Psalms 40:2
Psalms 41:1-2, 12
Psalms 47:1, 4-5
Psalms 56:9
Psalms 57:2-3
Psalms 59:16-17
Psalms 62:1-2
Psalms 91:15
Psalms 92:4
Psalms 107:6, 13, 14, 19-20
Psalms 108:13
Psalms 115:9-11
Psalms 124:8
Psalms 125:1
Psalms 138:7, 8
Psalms 145:19
Proverbs 24:19-20
Isaiah 25:8
Jeremiah 29:12-14
Jeremiah 31:9

Ezekiel 39:27-29
Daniel 3:17
Daniel 6:22-23
Obadiah 1:17
Nahum 1:7, 13
Zephaniah 3:20
Haggai 1:13
Zechariah 4:6
Zechariah 8:8
Zechariah 10:5
Matthew 7:7-8
Luke 11:9-10
John 15:4-5
Acts 7:9-10, 34
Acts 20:32
I Corinthians 10:13
Ephesians 1:19-21
Ephesians 3:20
Philippians 3:21
II Timothy 4:18
Hebrews 2:14
Hebrews 7:25
James 4:7-10
I Peter 1:5
Revelation 1:17-18

YOU ARE HEALED OF THE LORD

God Being with Us

Genesis 21:22
Genesis 26:3, 24
Genesis 28:15
Exodus 13:21-22
Numbers 6:24-26
Deuteronomy 1:29-30
Deuteronomy 4:29-31
Deuteronomy 9:3
Deuteronomy 10:14
Deuteronomy 20:3-4
Deuteronomy 31:6, 8
Joshua 1:5, 9
Joshua 21:44-45
I Samuel 2:8-9
I Samuel 3:19
II Samuel 7:3
II Samuel 22:2-4, 29-33
II Kings 6:16
I Chronicles 17:8
I Chronicles 28:9, 20
I Chronicles 29:11-12
II Chronicles 32:7-8
Ezra 8:31
Psalms 3:3-4
Psalms 9:10

Psalms 16:8
Psalms 18:6-17
Psalms 23:1-6
Psalms 33:18-19
Psalms 37:28
Psalms 41:12
Psalms 46:7
Psalms 62:1-2
Psalms 65:4
Psalms 68:19
Psalms 115:9-11
Psalms 139:1-18
Isaiah 58:11
Jeremiah 29:12-14
Jeremiah 31:1, 9
Jeremiah 32:40
Haggai 1:3
Zechariah 8:8
Zechariah 10:5
Matthew 7:7-8
Luke 11:9-10
John 15:4-5
I Corinthians 1:9
I Corinthians 10:13
Ephesians 1:19-21

CHAPTER 10: SCRIPTURES LISTS

Ephesians 3:20
Philippians 3:21

Revelation 1:17-18

Goodness of God

Deuteronomy 30:9
Joshua 23:14
Psalms 31:19
Psalms 34:8
Psalms 34:10B
Psalms 65:4
Psalms 68:19
Psalms 69:16
Psalms 73:1
Psalms 84:11
Psalms 85:12
Psalms 100:5
Psalms 106:1
Psalms 145:9
Jeremiah 32:40
Lamentations 3:25
Nahum 1:7
Galatians 3:29
James 1:17

Having Faith

Psalms 73:28
Psalms 118:8
Proverbs 3:5-6
Proverbs 29:25
Isaiah 64:4
Jeremiah 17:7-8
Lamentations 3:26
Zechariah 1:3
Matthew 6:8
Matthew 8:13
Matthew 9:28-29
Matthew 17:20
Matthew 18:18-20
Matthew 21:21-22
Mark 4:14-20
Mark 9:23
Luke 17:5-6
John 5:24
John 11:25
John 14:1, 12-14

YOU ARE HEALED OF THE LORD

John 20:31	Philippians 3:13-14
Acts 8:37	I Thessalonians 5:8
Acts 10:43	I Timothy 1:19
Romans 1:16-17	I Timothy 6:12
Romans 3:3-4	Hebrews 10:22-23
Romans 5:1	Hebrews 11:1, 6, 7-11, 20-33
Romans 9:33	
Romans 10:8-10, 17	Hebrews 12:2
Romans 12:3	Hebrews 13:9
I Corinthians 2:5	James 1:5-6
II Corinthians 5:7	James 2:17
Galatians 3:6	I Peter 2:6
Galatians 5:5-6	I John 5:4

Power and Authority of God and His Word

Genesis 28:15	II Samuel 22:31
Leviticus 26:3-12	I Kings 8:56
Numbers 23:19-20	I Chronicles 28:7
Deuteronomy 4:2	I Chronicles 29:11
Deuteronomy 7:9	II Chronicles 6:10
Deuteronomy 8:3	Nehemiah 9:6
Deuteronomy 30:9	Nehemiah 13:2
Deuteronomy 32:4	Job 37:23
Joshua 1:8	Psalms 8:6
Joshua 21:45	Psalms 12:6-7
II Samuel 7:25, 28-29	Psalms 18:6-17, 30

CHAPTER 10: SCRIPTURES LISTS

Psalms 19:7, 8, 11
Psalms 33:4, 6
Psalms 36:6
Psalms 46:9-10
Psalms 47:2
Psalms 89:34
Psalms 93:5
Psalms 95:4
Psalms 100:3
Psalms 105:8-10
Psalms 107:20
Psalms 111:5, 7
Psalms 119:9, 50, 74, 86, 89, 92, 93, 105, 114, 130, 140, 142, 144, 152, 160, 172
Psalms 138:2, 7
Psalms 145:6
Psalms 146:5-6
Psalms 147:5, 15
Proverbs 4:13, 20-23
Proverbs 6:23
Proverbs 23:11
Proverbs 30:5, 6
Ecclesiastic 8:5
Isaiah 11:4
Isaiah 12:6
Isaiah 25:8
Isaiah 28:16
Isaiah 29:14
Isaiah 34:16
Isaiah 39:8
Isaiah 40:28
Isaiah 44:24
Isaiah 45:19, 23
Isaiah 55:10-12
Isaiah 66:14
Jeremiah 1:12
Jeremiah 5:14
Jeremiah 10:10, 12-13
Jeremiah 23:29
Jeremiah 32:27
Jeremiah 51:15-16
Ezekiel 12:25
Daniel 6:26
Micah 2:7
Nahum 1:3-7
Zephaniah 3:16-17
Haggai 2:5
Zechariah 4:6
Malachi 3:6
Matthew 4:4
Matthew 5:18
Matthew 7:24

YOU ARE HEALED OF THE LORD

Matthew 19:26
Matthew 24:35
Matthew 28:18
Mark 4:39
Luke 1:37
Luke 4:4
Luke 8:11, 15
Luke 21:33
John 1:1-4, 14
John 5:24, 39
John 6:63
John 8:31-32
John 15:3, 7
John 17:17, 23
John 20:31
Romans 1:16
Romans 3:4
Romans 4:21
Romans 7:12
Romans 8:11
Romans 10:17
Romans 15:4
Ephesians 1:19-21
Ephesians 3:20
Ephesians 5:26
Ephesians 6:17
Philippians 1:6
Philippians 2:10-11, 16
Colossians 2:10
I Thessalonians 2:13
I Thessalonians 5:24
II Thessalonians 2:8
I Timothy 1:8
II Timothy 3:15, 16-17
Titus 1:2, 9
Hebrews 1:12
Hebrews 4:12
Hebrews 6:18
Hebrews 7:25
Hebrews 11:3
James 1:18
I Peter 1:25
II Peter 1:19, 21
Revelation 1:3, 16
Revelation 2:16
Revelation 22:19

CHAPTER 10: SCRIPTURES LISTS

Pray for Loved Ones (Insert the individuals name in the blank)

Psalms 1:1-4
Psalms 119:18
Psalms 129:4
John 17:14-17
Romans 6:12-14
Romans 8:2
Galatians 6:7
Galatians 5:24-26
Ephesians 5:11
Philippians 3:13-14
Philippians 3:21
Colossians 1:21-22
Colossians 3:1
Philemon 6
Hebrews 13:21
Hebrews 10:16
I John 2:15-18

Reasons and Benefits of Fasting

1. Directed by the Lord
Isaiah 58:5-6
Joel 2:12
II Corinthians 6:4-5
Matthew 9:15

2. Freedom, Deliverance, and Protection
Isaiah 58:6
Matthew 4:1-11
Matthew 17:20-21
Daniel 9:3-5

3. Healing
Isaiah 58:7-8
Matthew 17:20-21

4. The presence of the glory of God
   Isaiah 58:7-8
5. Answered prayers
   Isaiah 58:9
   Daniel 10:1-21
6. Guidance and Direction
   Isaiah 58:11
7. Building your faith
8. Cleansing your physical bodies

Wisdom and Guidance in your Healing Process

Exodus 24:7
Deuteronomy 4:10
Deuteronomy 8:3
Deuteronomy 32:11-12
Deuteronomy 33:3
Joshua 23:6
II Samuel 22:29, 33-34
I Chronicles 22:12
Nehemiah 8:13
Nehemiah 9:12
Psalms 5:8
Psalms 16:11
Psalms 23:2-3
Psalms 25:5, 9
Psalms 27:11, 13-14
Psalms 32:8
Psalms 34:10
Psalms 48:14
Psalms 73:24
Psalms 119:9, 30, 33, 66, 130, 133, 135, 144
Psalms 130:5
Psalms 138:8
Psalms 139:8-10
Psalms 143:10
Proverbs 3:4, 5-6, 7-8
Proverbs 4:5-6
Proverbs 6:23

CHAPTER 10: SCRIPTURES LISTS

Proverbs 9:10-11
Proverbs 20:24
Isaiah 2:3
Isaiah 11:2-3
Isaiah 30:21
Isaiah 42:16
Isaiah 43:18-19
Isaiah 44:2
Isaiah 48:17
Isaiah 58:11
Isaiah 63:14
Isaiah 64:8
Jeremiah 29:11-13
Jeremiah 31:9
Jeremiah 33:3, 6
Hosea 4:6a
Hosea 10:12
Amos 5:4
Habakkuk 2:2-3
Zechariah 1:3
Matthew 7:7-8
Matthew 13:54
Matthew 22:29

Mark 12:24
Luke 1:78-79
Luke 2:40
Luke 11:28
John 10:3-4
John 12:46
John 14:12
John 16:13
Romans 10:17
Romans 12:2
Romans 15:4
I Corinthians 1:5
I Corinthians 1:24
I Corinthians 2:16
II Corinthians 4:6
Ephesians 1:17-19
Philippians 2:5
Colossians 2:2-3
Colossians 3:16
Hebrews 13:9
James 1:5
James 3:17
James 4:2-3

www.ingramcontent.com/pod-product-compliance
Lightning Source LLC
Chambersburg PA
CBHW070108080526
44586CB00013B/1227